The Lost Decade:

★

Players *of the* 1970s
Cardinals

Gary W. Abbott

Susan M. DeFosset - Editor

Bluebird Publishing Co.
St. Louis, MO 63144
www.Bluebirdbookpub.com

★ *Dedication* ★

To Ed Mullen and Wally Thompson, who rode many a Redbird Express with me to Busch Stadium II, as well as Charlie Hamilton (check out Americaspastimetours.com) and Pat Rieck, who continue the tradition today in ballparks throughout the country.

To my home All-Star Team: Gail, tolerating the testosterone level in the household, always with patience and kindness, steady throughout, much like Ted Simmons in the 70's; Derek, as prolific with the guitar (and bass, piano, drums and vocals) as Lou Brock was with the bat (and legs) and Ryan, with a baseball swing as smooth as Keith Hernandez and a personality as large as Scipio Spinks.

And to my Dad, who introduced me to this great game. In the words of the Beatles Lennon/McCartney "In my life, I've loved them all".

★ *Introduction* ★

The St. Louis Cardinals enjoy a rich history of success, leading the National League with eleven world titles. From the Gashouse Gang in the '30's, the St. Louis Swifties in the '40's, the El Birdos of the late '60's, Whiteyball in the 1980's to the most remarkable titles in 2006 and 2011 under Tony LaRussa, the Cardinals indeed cemented their proud and rich history.

I attended my first game during the championship season of 1967 in the then "new" Busch Stadium with my local Cub Scout Pack, number 544 from the suburbs of St. Louis. What a great season to become a baseball fan for the first time! A World Championship resulted. I recall Bob Gibsons' sweat drenched face on the cover of The Sporting News that October, celebrating the Cardinals (and his) accomplishments.

The following season was even easier, running away from the pack to an easy league title with, once again, Gibson leading the way. The World Series seemed a cinch as well, leading three games to one against the American League Champ Detroit Tigers. Watching the seventh game of the series in the gymnasium of my grade school, the run was suddenly over- over for a long time, like fourteen years to be exact.

I continued to follow the team through those barren years of the '70's. I would catch the Redbird Express at Westroads (now The Gallaria) shopping center with my friends, meandering along Clayton Road to Skinker, then Lindell north to DeBaliviere, past the aged Stardust Theatre featuring Evelvn West and her $50,000 Treasure Chest on the marquee; I knew we weren't in the suburbs anymore. The bus lumbered past Delmar, into the fringes of north St. Louis. Past Cool Papa Bell Avenue, a street named for the Negro League legend and Hall of Famer. Finally, downtown was in sight: the Arch,

Stadium Cine, Lum's Restaurant (a personal favorite back in the day), and Busch Stadium.

The decade certainly had its share of highlights: a Gibson Cy Young and no-hitter, Brock's historic stolen base record, and Joe Torre and Keith Hernandez's MVP seasons. A division title however, was not one of them; only disappointment.

This is my tribute to all 228 players of that decade who wore the birds on the bat, some well known, many up for the proverbial cup-of-coffee. Listed in each brief baseball bio are how the player was acquired and departed, plus a brief synopsis of the player's career in baseball as well as with the Cardinals. In addition, the players post-baseball career is noted, if known. If you have any further information on any player from the decade, please reference The1970sCardinals@yahoo.com and feel free to add any accurate information.

The times became much brighter in Redbird Nation after the '70's. The Herzog and LaRussa eras closed the gap on one of the few unsuccessful decades in Cardinal history. In the words of the immortal Jack Buck, "Thanks for your time this time till next time."

Ted Abernathy

- May 29, 1970: Traded by the Chicago Cubs to the St. Louis Cardinals for Phil Gagliano.

- July 1, 1970: Traded by the St. Louis Cardinals to the Kansas City Royals for Chris Zachary.

Turning to a submarine delivery after a high school injury, Abernathy enjoyed a 14-year career in the majors, leading the National League in saves in both 1965 & 1967. His stay with the Cards was short-lived, only 11 games in a little over 1 month. The trade puzzled Ted. "I was pitching well for the Cardinals. I asked Bing Devine (G.M.) and he told me 'That's baseball, you move around'". Ted had two very good seasons with the Royals before ending his major league career at the conclusion of the 1972 season.

Ted later worked at Summey Building Systems in his native North Carolina as well as working with his son's landscaping business. Ted was involved in Baseball's alumni society as well as the Masons. Suffering from Alzheimer's, he passed away in December 2004 at 71.

Tommie Agee

- August 18, 1973: Traded by the Houston Astros to the St. Louis Cardinals for Dave Campbell and cash.

- December 5, 1973: Traded by the St. Louis Cardinals to the Los Angeles Dodgers for Pete Richert.

Tommie was in the last leg of his 12-year career with the Redbirds at the end of the 1973 season, hitting .177 with 3 home runs. A career .255 hitter, Agee had a great rookie year with the White Sox in 1966, earning Gold Glove, Rookie of the Year and All Star honors. He was a large part of the "Miracle Mets" of 1969, hitting the first home run in Met postseason history and making two circus catches in game three of the World Series.

After his career, Tommie coached youth baseball, owned a bar near Shea stadium, and later worked for a title insurance company. He died far too young of a heart attack in January 2001 at the age of 58.

Richard "Dick" Allen

- October 7, 1969: Traded by the Philadelphia Phillies with Jerry Johnson and Cookie Rojas to the St. Louis Cardinals for Byron Browne, Curt Flood, Joe Hoerner and Tim McCarver. Curt Flood refused to report to his new team. The St. Louis Cardinals sent Willie Montanez (April 8, 1970) and Jim Browning (minors) (August 30, 1970) to the Philadelphia Phillies to complete the trade.

- October 5, 1970: Traded by the St. Louis Cardinals to the Los Angeles Dodgers for Ted Sizemore and Bob Stinson.

A 7-time All Star, 1964 National League Rookie of the Year, 1972 A.L. MVP, Allen had a solid 15 year career, only interrupted by controversies throughout. After pleading with Phillie management and fans to trade him (scratching "boo", "trade me" in the infield dirt near first base), Dick was acquired by the Cards in the notorious trade involving Curt Flood. Greeted with a standing ovation in his inaugural game with the Redbirds, Dick had a solid season, batting .279 with 34 home runs and 101 RBI's, downgraded only by missing 40 games due to leg injuries.

His greatest success was accomplished with the White Sox, especially his 1972 MVP season.

Following a two year return to the Phillies, Allen ended his career in Oakland in 1977. In retirement, Dick has written (with Tim Whitaker) an autobiography titled Crash: The Life and Times of Dick Allen.

He has also been involved with the Phillies community relations department since the mid-1990's.

Ron Allen

- Before 1972 Season: Sent from the New York Mets to the St. Louis Cardinals in an unknown transaction.

A career minor leaguer, Ron had a brief stay with the Cards in 1972. Brother of former major leaguers Hank and Dick (Cardinal Class of 1970), he stated after his call up to the bigs, "I don't want four or five years in the majors. I just want one swing." He got his chance, slugging a home run, his only major league hit in 11 at bats. His career ended after that season.

A graduate of Youngstown State in 2010, and member of its Hall of Fame (1990), Ron lives in Maryland where he owns and trains race horses, one of his brother Dick's professions as well.

Mateo "Matty" Alou

- January 29, 1971: Traded by the Pittsburgh Pirates with George Brunet to the St. Louis Cardinals for Nelson Briles and Vic Davalillo.

- August 27, 1972: Traded by the St. Louis Cardinals to the Oakland Athletics for Steve Easton (minors) and Bill Voss.

- September 6, 1973: Purchased by the St. Louis Cardinals from the New York Yankees.

- October 25, 1973: Purchased by the San Diego Padres from the St. Louis Cardinals.

Matty, an excellent hitter (career .307 in 15 seasons) had two 300+ seasons with the team before being traded to Oakland for their pennant run. Part of the trio of Alou brothers (Felipe and Jesus), Matty was a two-time All Star who earned a World Series ring with the A's in 1972. He irritated Cardinal management by not reporting immediately to the team after being reacquired during the 1973 stretch run.

After his major league days were over, Matty played in Japan for three seasons before returning to his Dominican Republic home. There he coached and managed in the Dominican Winter League, as well as scouting for the Detroit and San Francisco organizations. A 2007 inductee to the Hispanic Heritage Baseball Hall of Fame, Alou died in November 2011 of complications from a stroke.

Luis Alvarado

- April 27, 1974: Traded by the Chicago White Sox to the St. Louis Cardinals for Ken Tatum.

- June 1, 1974: Traded by the St. Louis Cardinals with Ed Crosby to the Cleveland Indians for Jack Heidemann.

- May 27, 1975: Traded by the Cleveland Indians to the St. Louis Cardinals for a player to be named later. The St. Louis Cardinals sent Doug Howard (September 30, 1975) to the Cleveland Indians to complete the trade.

- November 6, 1976: Purchased by the Detroit Tigers from the St. Louis Cardinals.

Alvarado had two brief runs with the club, in 1974 & 1976. A career .214 hitter over 9 years, Luis was hampered by his light bat and erratic fielding in 1974. Luis managed a .286 average in '76 in limited duty. He ended his professional career by playing three seasons in Mexico (1979-1981). He was later linked to his native Puerto Rico, where he owned a grocery store. He died of an apparent heart attack in 2001 at the age of 52.

Garrabrant "Brant" Alyea

- May 18, 1972: Traded by the Oakland Athletics to the St. Louis Cardinals for Marty Martinez. Brant Alyea returned to original team on July 23, 1972.

From a career-best 1970 season with Minnesota (291, 16 HR, 61 RBI) Brant's career was near the end by the time of his arrival in St. Louis in 1972. After 3 hits in 19 at bats and 1 RBI, Alyea was sent back to Oakland where he won a World Series that year (even though he didn't play).

After his baseball career ended in 1973, Brant tended bar, sold insurance, and worked at the Tropicana Casino in Atlantic City, New Jersey. Brant, who fathered a child in Nicaragua during his winter league years, was finally reunited with his son after more than eighteen years. Brant Jr. was a minor leaguer who reached as high as AAA in 1988.

Dwain Anderson

- May 15, 1972: Traded by the Oakland Athletics to the St. Louis Cardinals for Don Shaw.

- June 7, 1973: Traded by the St. Louis Cardinals to the San Diego Padres for Dave Campbell.

Anderson, a veteran of the Oakland organization, was acquired the same week as Bernie Carbo in 1972. Dwain had a brief opportunity to secure the shortstop position after the departure of Dal Maxvill, batting .267 in 135 at bats. His opportunity pretty much ended after breaking a bone in his hand during batting practice. He was beaten out of the starting job in 1973 by the arrival of Ray Busse and eventually Mike Tyson. His career ended a year later in Cleveland.

Mike Anderson

- December 9, 1975: Traded by the Philadelphia Phillies to the St. Louis Cardinals for Ron Reed.

- March 28, 1978: Released by the St. Louis Cardinals.

An excellent fielding outfielder, Anderson provided some spark to a poor 1976 Redbird team. Appearing in 85 games, Mike batted a career- high .291 in 230 at bats, well above his career .246 mark. The following season wasn't as successful however, batting .221 in 169 at bats. He was released near the end of spring training the following year. Mike enjoyed only one season, with Philadelphia in 1974 where he batted more than 271 times, hitting .251 with 34 RBIs'.
Brother of Kent, an infielder with the Angels 1989-90, Mike ended his nine-year career in the majors in 1979 reuniting with the Phillies. He moved back to his native South Carolina, where he coached high school baseball and basketball.

John Andrews

- Before 1971 Season: Signed by the St. Louis Cardinals as an amateur free agent.

- December 6, 1973: Traded by the St. Louis Cardinals to the California Angels for Jeff Torborg.

A non-roster invitee in spring training of 1973, John made the opening day roster. A three-time draftee by other organizations, Andrews appeared in 16 games, allowing 18 hits with a 1-1 record. His professional career ended in the minor leagues after 1977. Andrews aspired to teach and coach high school baseball after the conclusion of his career.

Rudy Arroyo

- January 17, 1970: Drafted by the St. Louis Cardinals in the 4th round of the 1970 amateur draft (January Secondary).

- October 26, 1972: Traded by the St. Louis Cardinals with Greg Millikan (minors) to the Los Angeles Dodgers for Larry Hisle.

Called up to the Cardinals in 1971 due to injuries and ineffectiveness, Arroyo pitched in 9 games that season, all in relief. The southpaw, only 20 at the time of his promotion, struggled, giving up 18 hits in 11 2/3 innings, 2 homers, and a 0-1 record and 5.40 ERA. Rudy later made the Dodgers 1973 40-man roster but never appeared in the majors again. His professional career ended back in the Cardinals single A league.

His son Spencer, also a lefty, is currently pitching in the White Sox AA organization.

Benny Ayala

- March 30, 1977: Traded by the New York Mets to the St. Louis Cardinals for Doug Clarey.

- January 16, 1979: Traded by the St. Louis Cardinals to the Baltimore Orioles for Mike Dimmel.

A platoon outfielder known for his six seasons in Baltimore, Benny became the first New York Met to homer in their first at bat with the team. His stay with the Cardinals consisted of one game in 1977, 1 for 3, his hit a single off future Hall of Famer Steve Carlton. The ten year veteran batted a career .251, his best season being 1982 where he hit .305 with 6 homers and 24 RBI's.

He won a World Series Ring with the C's the following year. Ayala retired after the 1985 season. He is currently involved with the Baseball Assistance Team (BAT), serving as a liaison to his native Puerto Rico.

Ray Bare

- February 1, 1969: Drafted by the St. Louis Cardinals in the 3rd round of the 1969 amateur draft (January Secondary).
- April 4, 1975: Selected off waivers by the Detroit Tigers from the St. Louis Cardinals.

Ray had a brief run with the Redbirds in parts of 1972 & 74, appearing in 24 games with a 1-3 record over 41 innings. Upon his acquisition by the pitching-poor Tigers in 1975, Ray started 21 games in both 1975 & 76. The highlight of his career had to be his 2 hit shutout that stopped the Tigers 19 game losing streak in 1975. He also hurled two shutouts the following season. His professional career ended after the 1978 season with a major league mark of 16-26, with a 4.79 ERA. Ray lost his battle to leukemia in 1994 at the age of 44.

Mike Barlow

- May 23, 1975: the Oakland Athletics sent Mike Barlow to the St. Louis Cardinals to complete an earlier deal made on May 18, 1975. May 18, 1975: The Oakland Athletics sent a player to be named later and Steve Staniland (minors) to the St. Louis Cardinals for Ted Martinez.

- September 30, 1975: the St. Louis Cardinals sent Mike Barlow to the Houston Astros to complete an earlier deal made on June 25, 1975.

- June 25, 1975: The St. Louis Cardinals sent a player to be named later to the Houston Astros for Mike Easler.

A tall (6'6") relief pitcher, Mike lasted parts of seven seasons in the majors from 1975-1981. He made his first major league appearance with the Cardinals in 1975 at the age of 27, involved in nine games covering 7 2/3 innings during the season. He was part of the 1979 division-winning California Angels, with the second most innings pitched in relief for the squad. He ended his major league career with a 10-6 record and 4.63 ERA.

Born in Oneonta, New York, near Cooperstown, Mike graduated from Syracuse University with a degree in Economics. He later became athletic director at a junior/senior high school in the area. He was also involved in the Syracuse basketball broadcasts as a color commentator.

Jim Beauchamp

- Before 1958 Season: Signed by the St. Louis Cardinals as an amateur free agent.

- February 17, 1964: Traded by the St. Louis Cardinals with Chuck Taylor to the Houston Colt .45's for Carl Warwick.

- June 13, 1970: Traded by the Houston Astros with Leon McFadden to the St. Louis Cardinals for George Culver.

- October 18, 1971: Traded by the St. Louis Cardinals with Chip Coulter, Harry Parker and Chuck Taylor to the New York

Mets for Jim Bibby, Rich Folkers, Charlie Hudson and Art Shamsky.

An original signee by the Cardinals in 1958, Beauchamp enjoyed a 50-year career in baseball playing, managing and coaching. After only three at bats with the Redbirds in 1963, he eventually returned to the club as a part-time first baseman, outfielder, and a decent pinch hitter, batting .259 & .235 in 1970/71. A reserve his entire ten year career, Beauchamp hit .231 for his career, with only one season of 150 or more at bats. After his major league career ended after his appearance with the Mets in the 1973 World Series, Jim turned to managing in the minor leagues. After a long tenure (1975-1990) in managing, Jim joined the Braves from 1991-1998, earning a World Series title with the team in 1995.

Jim died in December 2007 from leukemia, the Braves honoring his memory by wearing a uniform patch the following season with his nickname "Beach".

Frank Bertaina

- August 14, 1970: Purchased by the St. Louis Cardinals from the Baltimore Orioles.

A member of the 1966 World Champion Baltimore Orioles, Bertaina wound up his 7 year major league career with the Cardinals in 1970. Frank started 5 games late that season, compiling a 1-3 record and 3.16 ERA over 31 innings. He frustrated Cardinals management in 1971 by saying he was not ready to pitch, ending in his demotion to AAA Tulsa.

Frank was later co-owner and founder of Fishing International (a sport fishing travel company) and the Lava Creek Lodge in California. One of Frank's favorite quotes, "Get your casts in while you can" summed up his passion for the sport. He passed away of a heart attack in 2010 at 65.

Jim Bibby

- October 18, 1971: Traded by the New York Mets with Rich Folkers, Charlie Hudson and Art Shamsky to the St. Louis Cardinals for Jim Beauchamp, Chip Coulter, Harry Parker and Chuck Taylor.

- June 6, 1973: Traded by the St. Louis Cardinals to the Texas Rangers for Mike Nagy and John Wockenfuss.

- June 9, 1984: Signed as a Free Agent with the St. Louis Cardinals.

- July 1, 1984: Released by the St. Louis Cardinals.

Bibby began his 12 year major league career with 12 appearances with the Cards in 1972-73. Traded to Texas in June, 1973 Jim pitched the first no-hitter in Texas Rangers history against the World Champion A's. A hard throwing, inconsistent starter who won 111 major league games, he enjoyed his greatest success with the Pirates, earning a World Series ring in 1979 and All Star appearance the following season with a 19-6 mark. Brother of UCLA basketball legend Henry, Bibby returned to his native Virginia as pitching coach for minor league Lynchburg for 15 years. Jim passed away at age 65 from bone cancer in 2010.

Dick Billings

- August 12, 1974: Purchased by the St. Louis Cardinals from the Texas Rangers.

- September 29, 1975: Released by the St. Louis Cardinals.

_One of the original Texas Rangers, Billings began his 8-year career with the Senators in 1968. His only seasons appearing in over 100 games, 1971 & 72, he hit .246 & .254 with 48 and 58 RBI's respectively. His biggest claim to fame is catching all 20 innings of a Senators game in 1971. With Simmons behind the plate for the Redbirds, Billings played in only 4 games in short trials in 1974 & 75, batting .125 in eight at bats. He retired after the season concluded with a career .227 average.

Dick moved back to Texas, working in the front office in group sales from 1989 to 1992. Both Dick and his wife are now real estate brokers in Arlington.

Rick Bosetti

- June 15, 1977: Traded by the Philadelphia Phillies with Dane Iorg and Tom Underwood to the St. Louis Cardinals for Bake McBride and Steve Waterbury.

- March 15, 1978: Traded by the St. Louis Cardinals to the Toronto Blue Jays for Tom Bruno and cash.

A line drive hitter with good defensive skills, Bosetti played in 41 games with the Cardinals in 1977, batting .232 with 3 RBI's. His only seasons as a starter were the following two seasons in Toronto, batting .259 & .260 with 42 and 65 RBI's respectively. His seven year career in the majors ended at age 28, batting .250 overall. He is notoriously known to have urinated in the outfield of every American League Park. Really!?!

With such a renowned reputation it is not a huge stretch that he later went into local politics. After 20 years as owner/partner of a system technology firm, Team Solutions, Rick went into public service in his native Redding, California. From 10 years as planning commissioner to two-time elected mayor (2008 & 2012), Rick has contributed greatly to his hometown. He has also served as head baseball coach at Simpson College.

Charles "Buddy" Bradford

- June 30, 1975: Traded by the Chicago White Sox to the St. Louis Cardinals for a player to be named later and cash. The St. Louis Cardinals sent Bill Parsons (July 7, 1975) to the Chicago White Sox to complete the trade.

- December 12, 1975: Traded by the St. Louis Cardinals with Greg Terlecky to the Chicago White Sox for Lee Richard.

Bradford had a solid half season for the Redbirds in 1975, primarily as a fourth outfielder and pinch hitter. Especially good against lefties, Bradford batted .272 with 4 homers and 15 RBI's with the club. At one point in the 1975 season, Buddy had only 29 hits but 30 RBI's. The fourth White Sox batter to hit one over the roof at old Comiskey Park (1969), Bradford was reacquired by the Sox for the third time in his career after the season. After one season in Japan in 1977 where he tore his hamstring, Buddy called it quits for good, ending with a career .226 average over 11 seasons.

A very astute investor during his playing days, Buddy became a bail officer and worked in security before working in the Cubs organization as a roving instructor in the minor leagues. In 1994 Buddy launched C & P Investments, which acquires apartments in the Los Angeles area.

Nelson Briles

- Before 1963 Season: Signed by the St. Louis Cardinals as an amateur free agent.

- January 29, 1971: Traded by the St. Louis Cardinals with Vic Davalillo to the Pittsburgh Pirates for Matty Alou and George Brunet.

A well regarded teammate and individual, Briles contributed greatly to the El Birdos World Series title in 1967, taking over the starting role in Gibson's absence. Traded after a injury-plagued 1970 season, Briles pitched a two-hitter against the Orioles in a do or die Game 5, winning another Series ring in the process. Following a 14 year, 129 win career, Nellie became a broadcaster with the Pirates for two years, followed by stints with the USA network and the Mariners. He returned to the Bucs in 1986 for a long role as director of corporate sales and established the Pirate Alumni Association.

An accomplished singer, Nellie sang the national anthem before Game 4 of the 1973 World Series. He died in February 2005 from a heart attack. He was 61.

Ed Brinkman

- November 18, 1974: Traded by the San Diego Padres with a player to be named later to the St. Louis Cardinals for Rich Folkers, Alan Foster and Sonny Siebert. The San Diego Padres sent Danny Breeden (December 10, 1974) to the St. Louis Cardinals to complete the trade.

- June 4, 1975: Traded by the St. Louis Cardinals with Tommy Moore to the Texas Rangers for Willie Davis.

Installed as the starting shortstop for the 1975 Cardinals, Brinkman came to the club with a light bat but solid glove. With the former Gold Glove Winner (1972) and All Star (1973) Ed provided stability with young players on the corners (Reitz and Hernandez). The artificial turf at Busch Stadium and many other parks in the National League were too fast for an aging vet. His 15-year career ended later that season with the Yankees with a .224 career average.

Brinkman soon went into coaching in the Detroit organization, including a year with the Tigers in 1979. He later was coach and scout for the White Sox, including part of Tony LaRussa's staff from 1983-1986. He retired from the organization in 2000. In 2008, Ed died at the age of 66 of heart problems and lung cancer.

Lou Brock

- June 15, 1964: Traded by the Chicago Cubs with Jack Spring and Paul Toth to the St. Louis Cardinals for Ernie Broglio, Doug Clemens and Bobby Shantz.

The Cardinals, beneficiaries of one of the most lopsided trades in history, acquired Lou in 1964. He helped lead them to a title that year, as well as 1967 and almost another the following year. One-hundred eighteen stolen bases in 1974, 938 for his career, Lou was the face of the franchise during the 1970's, even lending his name to the "Brockabrella", a clear, reverse tulip-shaped umbrella that allowed fans to stay in their seats during rainfalls. Lou enjoyed four 200+ hit seasons as well as 8 seasons hitting over .300.

My lasting memory of Lou was shortly after the 1967 World Series victory. Lou was honored by the city of Rock Hill, Missouri , where he, as well as my family, resided at the time. With Lou 's young son sliding across the stage just like his dad, I was able to secure an autograph and handshake from the star. I told my dad later that I would never wash my hand again after that encounter; since I was nine at the time, I probably didn't for a while.

Brock was elected to the Hall of Fame in 1985. He assists the Cards in spring training now and, along with his wife, ministers at the Abundant Life Fellowship Church in the St. Louis area.

George Brunet

- January 29, 1971: Traded by the Pittsburgh Pirates with Matty Alou to the St. Louis Cardinals for Nelson Briles and Vic Davalillo.

- May 10, 1971: Released by the St. Louis Cardinals.

Brunet, in his eighteenth year of professional baseball, pitched in only 7 games with the club in 1971 covering 9 innings before given his release. A colorful member of the Seattle Pilots, he is quoted in Jim Boutons' Ball Four as not ever wearing underwear because, " I don't have to worry about losing them." In 1973 he went south to Mexico, where he pitched until 1985 when he was 50 years old! Holder of the minor league record for strikeouts (3175) between his minor, major and Mexican league career, it is estimated he had 6000 strikeouts in his 32 year career.

Brunet remained in Mexico after his retirement from pitching, coaching, managing and conducting clinics. He died of a heart attack in 1991 at the young age of 56.

Tom Bruno

- March 15, 1978: Traded by the Toronto Blue Jays with cash to the St. Louis Cardinals for Rick Bosetti.

- March 31, 1980: Released by the St. Louis Cardinals.

Appearing in 18 games with the Cardinals in 1978, Bruno finished with a 4-3 mark, 1.99 ERA, winning two of his three starts. After being unscored on in his first seven appearances with the club in 1979, Bruno dropped significantly after that, to a 2-3 mark and 4.23 ERA. He ended his partial four year career at 7-7 with a 4.22 ERA. He was released in March 1980, one day short of qualifying for a partial Major League Baseball pension. He, as well as numerous others in that era, received a $10,000.00 settlement in lieu of the pension.

Always an outdoor lover, Bruno enjoyed a 12-year career as a pro fisherman before starting Major League Adventures in 1993, a hunting and fishing guide service and outfitting service in South Dakota.

Ron Bryant

- May 9, 1975: Traded by the San Francisco Giants to the St. Louis Cardinals for Luis Gonzalez (minors) and Larry Herndon.

- July 31, 1975: Released by the St. Louis Cardinals.

Much like Scipio Spinks of the '72 Cards, Ron Bryant bought a stuffed bear and named it "Bear Bryant" in an effort to improve his luck with the Giants that season. It worked. Winning 14 games in '72, Bryant had a career-year the following season with 24 victories and The Sporting New N.L. Pitcher of the Year award.

It all collapsed the following spring. Late at night during spring training Ron, who admitted having alcohol problems, jumped or fell into the side of a pool, hurting his back and requiring 30+ stitches on his side. He dropped to 3-15 in 1974 with a 5.61 ERA.

After briefly retiring in spring training 1975 and buying a restaurant in Arizona, the Cardinals gambled on Bryant resuming his '72-73 form, trading prospect Larry Herndon in the process. He did not, resulting in a 16.62 ERA over 8 2/3 innings, 20 hits allowed over 10 games. He ended his career that season with 57 major league wins.

Bob Burda

- Before 1958 Season: Signed by the St. Louis Cardinals as an amateur free agent.

- February 14, 1963: Traded by the St. Louis Cardinals to the Pittsburgh Pirates for Cal Neeman.

- February 2, 1971: Traded by the Milwaukee Brewers to the St. Louis Cardinals for Fred Reahm (minors).

- March 20, 1972: Traded by the St. Louis Cardinals to the Boston Red Sox for Mike Fiore.

A native St. Louisan, Burda was signed by the Redbirds in 1958 and made his major league debut with the club in 1962. Making his return to St. Louis 9 years later, Burda had a great season as a pinch hitter, batting .296 and leading the league in pinch hits with 14.

With a fine season as a left-handed batter off the bench, Burda was traded to Boston the following spring, his last in professional baseball. Burda ended his career with a .224 mark, with only two seasons of 200+ at bats.

Ray Busse

- November 28, 1972: Traded by the Houston Astros with Bobby Fenwick to the St. Louis Cardinals for Skip Jutze and Milt Ramirez.

- June 8, 1973: Traded by the St. Louis Cardinals to the Houston Astros for Stan Papi.

Rated the top prospect in the minors by Bob Kennedy, the Cardinals director of player development, Busse had a strong start in the Astros AAA with a .271 average and 13 homers in 1971. 1972 was tragic for Ray, losing his father to suicide as well as suffering a shoulder injury. After being acquired by the Cardinals, the spring training leader in RBI's with 11 in 1973, big things were expected of Ray Busse. The starting shortstop opening day with "pop in his bat", according to Astros former manager Harry Walker, Ray hit .143 with 11 errors in 24 games before being replaced by Mike Tyson. "Tight as a drum," according to one teammate, Ray was quickly returned to Houston two months later. His major league career ended the following season with a career average of .148 and 23 career hits. Ray now operates a landscaping company in Florida.

Dave Campbell

- June 7, 1973: Traded by the San Diego Padres to the St. Louis Cardinals for Dwain Anderson.
- August 18, 1973: Traded by the St. Louis Cardinals with cash to the Houston Astros for Tommie Agee.

With the exception of the 1970 season with the Padres, "Soup" was a backup infielder for his 8 year major league career, batting a career .213. Mired in the middle of a horrific batting slump that reached 0 for 45, Dave was hitless in 21 at bats for the Cardinals in 1973.

After a short managing stint when his career ended in 1974, Dave has enjoyed a 30+ year career in broadcasting. Campbell has broadcast games for the Padres, Rockies, San Diego State sports teams, as well as his role as baseball analyst on ESPN.

James Campbell

- January 14, 1970: Purchased by the St. Louis Cardinals from the Baltimore Orioles.
- October 21, 1970: Traded by the St. Louis Cardinals to the Boston Red Sox for Dick Schofield
-

Campbell enjoyed his only taste of the majors in 1970, appearing at the plate 13 times, all as a pinch-hitter with 3 hits and a RBI. His 10 year minor league career ended the following season.

Sal Campisi

- Before 1964 Season: Signed by the St. Louis Cardinals as an amateur free agent.
- October 20, 1970: Traded by the St. Louis Cardinals with Jim Kennedy to the Minnesota Twins for Charlie Wissler (minors) and Herman Hill.

Sal, a Brooklyn New York native, had a fine minor league career with the Cardinals organization, winning 10 or more games five times. Campisi had a good 1970 season with the Redbirds, appearing in 37 games with 4 saves and a 2.92 ERA, but 37 walks. Sal injured his back during the season and was not the same afterward. He was traded to Minnesota at the end of the season. He pitched only 4 more innings in the bigs after August 28, 1970.

A member of the Long Island University Hall of Fame, Sal now lives in Florida where his family owns a auto dealership.

Doug Capilla

- December 3, 1973: Drafted by the St. Louis Cardinals from the San Francisco Giants in the 1973 rule 5 draft.
- June 15, 1977: Traded by the St. Louis Cardinals to the Cincinnati Reds for Rawly Eastwick.

A lefty with a good fastball and curve, Capilla was never able to put it all together in the majors. Doug, one of 37 Hawaiian- born major leaguers (see Ryan Kurosaki) pitched in nine games with the Redbirds from 1976-'77, leaving with a 1-0 record and 7.59 ERA in nine games covering 10 2/3 innings. Dougs' sister was married to the Texas Rangers' Bump Wills. He became a spot starter with the Reds, sporting a 7-8 record in 1977, however he won only four more major league games after, ending his career in 1981 with a career 12-18 record.

Bernie Carbo

- May 19, 1972: Traded by the Cincinnati Reds to the St. Louis Cardinals for Joe Hague.
- October 26, 1973: Traded by the St. Louis Cardinals with Rick Wise to the Boston Red Sox for Reggie Smith and Ken Tatum.
- March 10, 1979: Signed as a Free Agent with the St. Louis Cardinals.
- May 27, 1980: Released by the St. Louis Cardinals.

Carbo, The Sporting News National League Rookie of the Year in 1970 played for the Redbirds in 1972 & 73, hitting .286 in 1973. By then, drug use began to take its toll on his body. "I was a drug addict and alcoholic for 28 years. There wasn't much that I didn't do." Traded to Boston (along with Mighty Joe Young, see Spinks) Bernie was part of the historic 1975 game 6, homering to tie the game in the bottom of the eighth.

Following the end of his twelve-year career (.264 average), which included another stop in St. Louis (1979 & 1980), Carbo went to cosmetology school and operated a hair salon for eight years. Former Boston teammates Ferguson Jenkins and Bill Lee helped him find the Baseball Assistance Team, instrumental in helping him recover from his addictions. Bernie later formed the Diamond Club Ministry, in which he speaks to young adults about religion, baseball and the dangers of substance abuse.

Jose Cardenal

- November 21, 1969: Traded by the Cleveland Indians to the St. Louis Cardinals for Vada Pinson.
- July 29, 1971: Traded by the St. Louis Cardinals with Bob Reynolds and Dick Schofield to the Milwaukee Brewers for Charlie Loseth (minors) and Ted Kubiak.

Jose, a Cardinal for 1970 and part of 1971, had a great first season for the club, hitting .293 with 10 homers and 74 RBI's.

A career lasting 18 years, the Cuban native had a career .275 average with 1913 hits. With the club looking for spots for younger teammates Jose Cruz and Luis Melendez, Jose was traded to Milwaukee the next year.

After his career ended at the conclusion of the 1980 season, and his only World Series appearance with Kansas City, Jose coached in the big leagues for the Reds, Cardinals (1994 & 95) and Yankees (1996-1999), earning 2 World Series rings in the process. He later worked in the Washington organization as senior advisor to the general manager from 2005-09.

Steve Carlton

- October 8, 1963: Signed by the St. Louis Cardinals as an amateur free agent.
- February 25, 1972: Traded by the St. Louis Cardinals to the Philadelphia Phillies for Rick Wise.

"Lefty" achieved the first of his 6 20-game winning seasons in 1971 after almost losing 20 games (19) in 1970. The first pitcher to strike out 19 batters in a 9-inning game (against the Mets in 1969) , Carlton was embroiled in a bitter contract dispute with August Busch and the Cardinals. Steve was traded for Rick Wise of the Phillies. While most people at the time claimed the trade even, Carlton, with his momentous career, soon turned the deal into one of the worst for the Redbirds.

A four-time Cy Young Award winner (72, 77, 80 & 82), 329 career wins, a 27 win season, a 10-time All Star over 24 years, Steve was elected to the Hall of Fame in 1994.

Now retired on his 400 acre ranch in Colorado, Carlton books appearances and sells memorabilia through his website of the same name.

Clay Carroll

- March 23, 1977: Traded by the Chicago White Sox to the St. Louis Cardinals for Lerrin LaGrow.
- August 31, 1977: Traded by the St. Louis Cardinals to the Chicago White Sox for players to be named later. The Chicago White Sox sent Nyls Nyman (September 2, 1977), Dave Hamilton (November 28, 1977) and Silvio Martinez (November 28, 1977) to the St. Louis Cardinals to complete the trade.

A reliable relief pitcher, Carroll was a vital part of the Reds "Big Red Machine" of the 1970's, earning a World Series ring in 1975. An All Star in 1971 & '72, Clay held the title of most National League saves with 37 in '72, a record he held until Bruce Sutter of the Cards broke it with 45 in 1984.

Clay was the most reliable relief pitcher out of the pen in 1977 with a 4-2 record, 2.50 ERA, and 4 saves covering 90 innings. He was dealt back to the White Sox in September because of his advancing age (36) and hefty salary.

His career ended after 1978 with a 96-73 record, a 2.94 ERA and 143 career saves. Clay was elected to the Cincinnati Reds Hall of Fame in 1979 as well as the Alabama Sports Hall of Fame in 1992.

Danny Cater

- March 29, 1975: Traded by the Boston Red Sox to the St. Louis Cardinals for Danny Godby.

In the last of his 12-year career, Cater had only 35 at bats with the Cardinals, batting .229 before being dropped by the club in June 1975, ending with a respectable .276 career average. Prior to the Cardinals, Danny was probably known for two things: runner-up to Carl Yastrzemski for A.L. Batting title in 1968 at a .290 average, and traded by the Yankees to the Red Sox for fireman Sparky Lyle. The trade did not go well for Sox fans.

After retirement from the game; Danny was the hitting instructor for the Yankees AAA Syracuse team one season, winning the league title that season. After a new management team came in, Danny moved back to his native Texas. He has been employed since 1977 by the State of Texas in the Comptroller of Public Accounts, contacting tax delinquent businesses.

Charlie Chant

- October 28, 1975: Traded by the Oakland Athletics to the St. Louis Cardinals for Larry Lintz.

Not to be confused with the fictional Chinese-American detective, this number one son played briefly for the Cardinals in 1976. Appearing in 15 games that season, Charlie batted .143 in 14 of his 19 career at bats. The outfielder ended his career with the Cardinals AAA team in New Orleans in 1977, where he was a teammate of future Cardinal manager Tony LaRussa.

Bob Chlupsa

- June 6, 1967: Drafted by the St. Louis Cardinals in the 5th round of the 1967 amateur draft (June Secondary).
- June 20, 1972: Traded by the St. Louis Cardinals with Mike Fiore to the San Diego Padres for Rafael Robles. Mike Fiore returned to original team on July 3, 1972.
-

A 6'7" righthander, Chlupsa (pronounced (CLUP-sa) had a 15-game career in the majors, all with the Cardinals in 1970 and 71. His 0-2 record and 8.84 career ERA did not reflect his overall athleticism. Bob was a two-sport athlete at Manhattan College (where he is a Hall of Fame member), and a draft choice of the San Diego Rockets basketball team in 1967.

Upon his retirement from the game after two minor league seasons in Hawaii, Bob has worked in sales and marketing for over 35 years.

Doug Clarey

- December 2, 1974: Drafted by the St. Louis Cardinals from the Minnesota Twins in the 1974 minor league draft.
- March 30, 1977: Traded by the St. Louis Cardinals to the New York Mets for Benny Ayala.

With Mike Tyson ailing and Mario Guerrero and Luis Alvarado in AAA Tulsa needing to clear waivers, Clarey was called up from A ball to provide backup briefly in 1976. Pinch hitting in the 16th inning at San Francisco, Cleary hit a game-winning home run, one of only 7 players to homer in 5 or fewer major league appearances. Doug was honored the following homestand and presented a watch to commemorate the feat. His major league career ended that season, one for four with the home run.

Doug earned his real estate license after baseball, dealing in commercial real estate in California until 1993. He entered the pizza business thereafter, owning and operating Cheech's Pizza in the Los Angeles area.

Lance Clemons

- April 15, 1972: Traded by the Houston Astros with Scipio Spinks to the St. Louis Cardinals for Jerry Reuss.
- March 29, 1973: the St. Louis Cardinals sent Lance Clemons to the Boston Red Sox to complete an earlier deal made on January 24, 1973.
- January 24, 1973: The St. Louis Cardinals sent a player to be named later to the Boston Red Sox for Mike Nagy.

Clemons had a brief major league career, appearing in 19 games and 35 innings, primarily with Kansas City. The lefty was in three games with the Redbirds in 1972, pitching 5 1/3 innings with a 0-1 record and 10.13 ERA.

After arm injuries halted his career after the 1975 season, Clemons turned to teaching and coaching at the high school level in Florida. Lance then worked at UPS for another twenty years before succumbing to cancer in 2008 at 60. His alma mater, West Chester University in Pennsylvania named an endowment scholarship in his honor.

Donn Clendenon

- December 9, 1971: Signed as a Free Agent with the St. Louis Cardinals.
- August 7, 1972: Released by the St. Louis Cardinals.

In the last of his 12-year career, Donn had a inglorious end with the Cardinals in 1972, batting .191 with 4 HR and 9 RBI's in a reserve role. Runner-up for National League Rookie of the Year in 1962, Donn enjoyed solid seasons with the Bucs from 1962-1966. He was MVP of the 1969 Miracle Mets World Series before enjoying his last solid season in 1970, batting .288, with 22 homers, 97 RBI's. He finished with a career .274 mark and 159 homers.

After working in personnel management after retirement, Donn earned his law degree in 1978 from Duquesne University. Donn practiced criminal law and later became a addiction counselor after battling drug issues himself. He died of leukemia in September 2005 at the age of 70.

Reggie Cleveland

- August 28, 1965: Signed by the St. Louis Cardinals as an amateur free agent.
- December 7, 1973: Traded by the St. Louis Cardinals with Terry Hughes and Diego Segui to the Boston Red Sox for John Curtis, Mike Garman and Lynn McGlothen.

Reggie, nicknamed "Double Cheeseburger" for his hefty physique, was a solid starter during his three full seasons with the Cardinals, winning between 12-14 games each season from 1971-73. Upon his trade to Boston, a clearly disappointed manager Red Schoendienst noted, "He's the best I got."

The first Canadian to start a World Series game (1975) Reggie won 105 games over his 13 year career, (and lost 106).

After his career, Reggie moved back to Canada and sold cars and real estate. From 1991-95 he worked in the Toronto organization as minor league pitching coach. A member of the Canadian Baseball Hall of Fame (1986), Cleveland at last look was selling luxury cars in the Dallas area.

Tony Cloninger

- March 24, 1972: Traded by the Cincinnati Reds to the St. Louis Cardinals for Julian Javier.
- July 26, 1972: Released by the St. Louis Cardinals.

Tony, at the end of his 12 year career, was a hard throwing righthander who had the distinction of being the only pitcher to hit two grand slams in one game. Cloninger, who won 113 games in his career, had back-to-back 19 and 24 win seasons with the Milwaukee Braves in 1964 & '65. He appeared in only 17 games with the Cardinals, with a 0-2 record and 5.19 ERA. Upon the end of his big league career, Tony briefly held a car sales position as well as working at a sporting goods store. According to Tony, "I never found the satisfaction that I got from baseball." In the late 1980's, Tony coached in the minor leagues before accepting the position of pitching coach for the New York Yankees in 1992. He earned four World Series rings with the Yanks (and a runner up in 2001 as well as with the 1970 Cincinnati Reds). After a successful bladder cancer battle, Tony enjoys life in the Denver area.

Bob Coluccio

- June 8, 1978: Traded by the Houston Astros to the St. Louis Cardinals for Frank Riccelli.
- October 2, 1978: Traded by the St. Louis Cardinals to the New York Mets for Paul Siebert.

The "Macaroni Pony", as named by the Milwaukee Brewers broadcast team was a draft pick of the Seattle Pilots in 1969. Bobs' best major league season was his first in 1973 where he batted .224 with 15 homers and 58 Ribbies. He is only one of five Brewers to hit a walk-off home run in the 14th inning or later, when he turned the trick in the 16th inning in April 1974. His production dropped off considerably after that, culminating in his final roundup with the Redbirds in 1978. He went 0 for 3 with the team before ending his career that season in AA Springfield. He left the bigs with a career .220 batting average.

Now living in California, Bob is a real estate agent in addition to giving batting lessons to high school and collegiate players in the Newport Beach area.

Willie Crawford

- March 2, 1976: Traded by the Los Angeles Dodgers to the St. Louis Cardinals for Ted Sizemore.
- October 20, 1976: Traded by the St. Louis Cardinals with John Curtis and Vic Harris to the San Francisco Giants for Mike Caldwell, John D'Acquisto and Dave Rader.

A talented outfielder, Crawford spent 12 of his 14 major league seasons with the Dodgers, earning a World Series ring in 1965. Usually the fourth outfielder, Crawfords' best seasons were in 1973 & '74 where he enjoyed back-to-back .295 seasons with 66 and 61 RBI's respectively. Crawford had a excellent season with the Redbirds in 1976, batting a career-high .304 with 9 homers and 50 RBI's. However, being the second oldest outfielder behind Lou Brock and a youth movement in place, Crawford was dealt to the Giants.

He ended his professional career with two seasons in the Mexican League (1978-1979) retiring with a .268 average. Crawford died of kidney disease in 2004 at the young age of 57.

Ed Crosby

- February 1, 1969: Drafted by the St. Louis Cardinals in the 2nd round of the 1969 amateur draft (January).
- July 27, 1973: Traded by the St. Louis Cardinals with Gene Dusen (minors) to the Cincinnati Reds for a player to be named later and Ed Sprague. The Cincinnati Reds sent Roe Skidmore (September 30, 1973) to the St. Louis Cardinals to complete the trade.
- March 29, 1974: Purchased by the St. Louis Cardinals from the Philadelphia Phillies.
- June 1, 1974: Traded by the St. Louis Cardinals with Luis Alvarado to the Cleveland Indians for Jack Heidemann.

Ed, a light-hitting backup infielder for the club between 1970 and 1973, hit a career best .253 in his first season. His 6 year career produced only 677 at bats and no home runs. A member of the Long Beach California Hall of Fame, Ed later became a scout, signing Long Beach University alum Jason Giambi. Ed is the father of former major leaguer Bobby Crosby, 2004 A.L. Rookie of the Year.

Cirilo "Tommy"Cruz

- Before 1969 Season: Signed by the St. Louis Cardinals as an amateur free agent.
- October 26, 1973: Traded by the St. Louis Cardinals with cash to the Texas Rangers for Sonny Siebert

Part of the trio of Cruz brothers, (Jose & Hector being the others), Tommy appeared in only 3 games with the Cardinals in 1973 with no plate appearances. Traded to Texas at the conclusion of the season, Tommy later appeared at the plate twice during a short stint with the White Sox in 1977. His career was extended by playing 6 seasons for Nippon in the Japanese Leagues. In 2009 Tommy was named hitting coach for the Mariners High Desert single A team.

Hector Cruz

- January 22, 1970: Signed by the St. Louis Cardinals as an amateur free agent.
- December 8, 1977: Traded by the St. Louis Cardinals with Dave Rader to the Chicago Cubs for Jerry Morales, Steve Swisher and cash.

HECTOR CRUZ   INFIELDER

Hector, the Sporting News Minor League Player of the Year in 1975, became the Cards starting third baseman the year following the trade of Ken Reitz. Cruz had a erratic season in his only full-time season, batting .228 with 13 home runs, an impressive 71 RBI's, but a league-leading 26 errors. Reitz returned to the team the following season; Hector was moved to the outfield where his numbers tumbled (.236, 6 HR, 42 RBI). He was traded to the Cubs, where his career ended with a .225 career average. In 1983 Hector joined brother Tommy in the Japanese League, eventually joining the Postal Service where he works as a mail carrier in Chicago.

Jose Cruz

- October 27, 1966: Signed by the St. Louis Cardinals as an amateur free agent.
- October 24, 1974: Purchased by the Houston Astros from the St. Louis Cardinals.

The most renowned of the Cruz brothers, Jose batted .274 in the second half of the 1971 season. A .235 and .227 seasons followed. With the 1974 outfield consisting of Lou Brock, Bake McBride and newly acquired Reggie Smith, Jose was primarily a part-timer. A .247 hitter for the Birds, Cruzs' career took off after being traded to Houston after the '74 season. A career .292 hitter with the Stros, and 1980 & 85 All Star, Jose has the distinction of appearing in all 9 Houston postseason appearances through the years; 3 as a player (1980, 81 & 86) and 6 as a coach (1997-99, 01, 04-05) . In his 29th year with the Astros, Jose is currently special assistant to the General Manager. His #25 was retired by the club in 1992.

George Culver

- November 5, 1969: Traded by the Cincinnati Reds to the St. Louis Cardinals for Ray Washburn.
- June 13, 1970: Traded by the St. Louis Cardinals to the Houston Astros for Jim Beauchamp and Leon McFadden.

Culver, who won his first three games as a Redbird, stumbled afterwards and ended his tenure with a 3-3 record and 4.61 ERA. A nine year veteran, his only season with double digit wins was in 1968, when he hurled a no-hitter. After his career ended in 1974 with a 48-49 record, 3.62 ERA (plus 1 year in Japan), George has managed in the California League, 18 years in the Phillies/Dodgers organization as AA & AA coach/manager. Bakersfield College in California has honored their beloved native with their baseball clubhouse named after George.

John Cumberland

- June 16, 1972: Traded by the San Francisco Giants to the St. Louis Cardinals for Jeff Mason (minors).
- November 29, 1972: Traded by the St. Louis Cardinals with Larry Hisle to the Minnesota Twins for Wayne Granger.

Another early 70's pitcher who did not work out, Cumberland had a very good season the year before with the Giants, a 9-6 record with a 2.92 ERA, including 2 shutouts. The left-hander pitched only 14 games, with one start, a 1-1 record with a 6.65 ERA before being traded at the end of the year. His big league career ended with 15 victories. John had his largest claim to fame after his retirement from pitching. After a six year stint as a minor league pitching coach, Cumberland made it back to the bigs as the Red Sox and later, Royals pitching coach/bullpen coach. His major league tenure ended in 2004.

John Curtis

- December 7, 1973: Traded by the Boston Red Sox with Mike Garman and Lynn McGlothen to the St. Louis Cardinals for Reggie Cleveland, Terry Hughes and Diego Segui.
- October 20, 1976: Traded by the St. Louis Cardinals with Willie Crawford and Vic Harris to the San Francisco Giants for Mike Caldwell, John D'Acquisto and Dave Rader.

One of the many left-handers the Cardinals tried in their rotation after trading Carlton and Reuss, Curtis pitched for the club between 1974 & 1976. His games started with the team dropped from a high of 29 in '74 (with 10 wins) down to 15 in 1976 (with 6 wins). He had occasional success out of the bullpen, especially in 1975. He ended his run with the team with a 24-34 record.

After his 15-year career ended in 1984 with a career 89-97 record, 3.96 ERA and 14 shutouts, Curtis, an English major at Clemson , turned to freelance writing. His articles have appeared in such publications as the Boston Globe, San Francisco Chronicle and Sports Illustrated. He also coached briefly in the Independent League Long Beach team in 2001 & 2002, where he makes his home.

Vic Davalillo

- May 30, 1969: Traded by the California Angels to the St. Louis Cardinals for Jim Hicks.
- January 29, 1971: Traded by the St. Louis Cardinals with Nelson Briles to the Pittsburgh Pirates for Matty Alou and George Brunet.
-

A career .279 hitter over 16 seasons, Davalillo enjoyed a excellent 1970 season, pinch-hitting in 74 games and compiling a .311 average and 33 RBIs. Vic's 23 pinch hits that season tied a National League record at the time. He also appeared in 2 games as a mop-up pitcher during the 1969 season, retiring none of the 4 batters he faced.

Davalillo won World Series rings with Pittsburgh (1971) and Oakland (1973) before retiring in 1980 at 43. Vic continued to play, first in the Mexican league (1981) and another 6 years in his native Venezuela. A member of the Venezuelan Baseball Hall of Fame (2003) Vic continues to teach his beloved sport in his homeland.

Jerry DaVanon

- June 7, 1966: Drafted by the St. Louis Cardinals in the 1st round (17th pick) of the 1966 amateur draft (June Secondary).
- October 14, 1968: Drafted by the San Diego Padres from the St. Louis Cardinals as the 24th pick in the 1968 expansion draft.
- May 22, 1969: Traded by the San Diego Padres with Bill Davis to the St. Louis Cardinals for Sonny Ruberto and John Sipin.
- November 30, 1970: Traded by the St. Louis Cardinals to the Baltimore Orioles for Moe Drabowsky.
- November 23, 1976: Traded by the Houston Astros with Larry Dierker to the St. Louis Cardinals for Bob Detherage and Joe Ferguson.
- May 11, 1977: Released by the St. Louis Cardinals.

Jerry, a original San Diego Padre and four-time Cardinal bounced around considerably during his 8-year career, a Cardinal during the 1969 & 70 seasons, 74 & 77 seasons. A .189 hitter for the Redbirds during his career, while at Houston in 1975 & 76 he batted a career high .278 & .290 respectively. His seasons with the Astros were the only ones where he had over 100 plate appearances in a season. He finished with a career .234 average in only 499 at bats.

Father of Jeff, a American Leaguer from 1999-2007, DaVanon retired to Houston, where he works in sales of specialty metal products. He has also refereed high school basketball for over 25 years.

Willie Davis

- June 4, 1975: Traded by the Texas Rangers to the St. Louis Cardinals for Ed Brinkman and Tommy Moore.
- October 20, 1975: Traded by the St. Louis Cardinals to the San Diego Padres for Dick Sharon

Acquired mid-season 1975, Willie provided a huge lift to the team with his great speed and solid hitting. Davis batted .291 with the Cards, with 6 home runs and 50 ribbies during his time with the team. A 14-year veteran of the Dodgers, Willie won Gold Gloves from 1971-'73 and made All Star Games in 1971 and '73. He helped the Dodgers win World Series titles in 1963 and 1965, though he does hold an inglorious record of making three errors on two consecutive plays in the 1966 World Series. He also holds the Dodgers record for longest hitting streak, 31, set in 1969.

After sitting out five games with the Cardinals due to a dispute with his ex-wife over garnishing wages and suggesting a 5-year million dollar contract (he was 35 at the time), Willie was traded after the season. His career ended in Mexico, where he managed a couple of seasons. He ended with a career .279 average over 14 seasons.

Plagued by financial difficulties throughout his career, Willie made headlines after he threatened to kill his parents and burn down their home if he was not paid $5,000. He was arrested but not charged. Willie was found dead at his home of natural causes in 2010 at the age of 69

John Denny

- June 4, 1970: Drafted by the St. Louis Cardinals in the 29th round of the 1970 amateur draft. Player signed June 19, 1970.
- December 7, 1979: Traded by the St. Louis Cardinals with Jerry Mumphrey to the Cleveland Indians for Bobby Bonds.

A valued member of the starting staff from 1975-79, Denny enjoyed three fine seasons with the Cardinals, the others being hampered by numerous leg and ankle injuries. After an initial rookie season in 1975 with 10 victories, Denny led the league the following season in ERA, with a 2.52 mark, along with 11 victories with little offensive support. His 1978 season was productive as well, resulting in a 14 win, 2.96 ERA.

After a few down seasons in Cleveland, Denny resurrected his career with the Phillies, earning the Cy Young Award (and Comeback Player of the Year) in 1983 based on his 19-6 record and 2.37 ERA. John finished his career in 1986 with 123 wins 13 years.

John has remained in sports, spending a year building a sports camp in St. Louis for the Fellowship of Christian Athletes, as well as a rehab coach for Arizona from 2001-2004, and earning a World Series ring as well. He currently runs JAD Baseball Experience in Memphis, teaching pitchers of all ages the finer points of the game.

John D'Acquisto

- October 20, 1976: Traded by the San Francisco Giants with Mike Caldwell and Dave Rader to the St. Louis Cardinals for Willie Crawford, John Curtis and Vic Harris.
- May 17, 1977: Traded by the St. Louis Cardinals with Pat Scanlon to the San Diego Padres for Butch Metzger.

The National League Rookie Pitcher of the Year in 1974 with San Francisco, D'Acquisto threw extremely fast (102.4 on radar), but wild. After elbow surgery and a 3-8 record in 1976, John was acquired by the Redbirds. Going on the disabled list before the second game of the season with a leg injury, John pitched in only 3 games covering 8 1/3 innings, 4 innings of those no-hit ball against Cincinnati. His career ended in 1982 with a 34-51 record, 4.56 ERA and almost as many walks as strikeouts.

A high school pitching coach and investment advisor after his playing days, John was later sentenced to almost 10 years in prison for defrauding investors, wire fraud and money laundering.

Fortunately, John turned his life around at that point, earning a Fire Science Degree and EMT training while in prison, earning an early release and coaching baseball again, including the U.S. Navy baseball team.

John later earned a Doctorate of Science in Exercise Science & Physiology and is currently director and consultant of a company that develops organic fertilizers and other products.

Larry Dierker

- November 23, 1976: Traded by the Houston Astros with Jerry DaVanon to the St. Louis Cardinals for Bob Detherage and Joe Ferguson.
- March 28, 1978: Released by the St. Louis Cardinals.

Associated with the Astro organization for almost 50 years, Dierker began his career as an eighteen-year-old in 1964. A two-time All Star, Larry pitched a no-hitter in his final season as a player with the Strohs in 1976, the first in Houston history.

Hampered by a broken ankle in spring training and shoulder problems afterward, Dierker did not become the veteran stopper the Cards were hoping for in 1977, his only season outside Houston. Larry finished the season with a 2-6 record, 4.58 ERA in 11 games covering only 39 1/3 innings. His career ended that season with a career 139 victories and 3.31 ERA, the best pitcher in the young Astros history to that point.

Larry soon became the color commentator on Astros broadcasts from 1979-1996, and 2004 & 2005. He then moved from the broadcast booth to the dugout, piloting the Astros from 1997-2001. Four of his five seasons resulted in playoff appearances, including N.L. Manager of the Year in 1998, the most successful managing career in Houston history. Larry was later involved in community outreach programs with the team before leaving the organization early in 2013.

Mike Dimmel

- January 16, 1979: Traded by the Baltimore Orioles to the St. Louis Cardinals for Benny Ayala.

A strong defensive outfielder and pinch runner, Dimmel toiled in the minors for eight seasons, seeing major league duty in 33 games with Baltimore in 1977 & '78. His last look in the bigs came with the Redbirds in 1979; he made the opening day roster due to Jerry Mumphrey starting the season on the DL. Mike got into six games with three at bats, one hit, one run scored and one caught stealing. He was sent down with Mumphreys' return, ending his professional career with AA Springfield the following year.

Mike is currently an investment advisor in the Dallas area.

Myron (Moe) Drabowsky

- October, 1965: Purchased by the St. Louis Cardinals from the Kansas City Athletics. (Date given is approximate. Exact date is uncertain.)
- November 29, 1965: Drafted by the Baltimore Orioles from the St. Louis Cardinals in the 1965 rule 5 draft.
- November 30, 1970: Traded by the Baltimore Orioles to the St. Louis Cardinals for Jerry DaVanon.
- August 8, 1972: Released by the St. Louis Cardinals.

The 17-year veteran was in his next to last season with the Cardinals in 1971, leading the team in saves with 8 and with a 6-1 record in 51 games. The following season his role was reduced by the acquisition of Diego Segui. A two-time World Champion (Orioles in 1966 &

1970) and member of the National Polish Hall of Fame, Moe was well known as a prankster. Slipping sneezing powder into the air- conditioning system of the opponent's locker room was a pet trick, as well as putting goldfish in the other team's water cooler. He was a master at hotfoots, lighting baseball commissioner Kuhns' shoe on fire during the Orioles' 1970 series victory. Snakes mysteriously appeared in shaving kits and lockers, to name a few.

After his career concluded in 1972 with a 88-105 record, Moe served as coach with both Chicago teams and worked with the Orioles as their pitching coach in Florida with players in extended spring training and rehab assignments. Moe passed away June 10, 2006 following a long battle with multiple myeloma at age 70.

Rob Dressler

- July 24, 1978: the San Francisco Giants sent Rob Dressler to the St. Louis Cardinals to complete an earlier deal made on July 18, 1978. July 18, 1978: The San Francisco Giants sent a player to be named later to the St. Louis Cardinals for John Tamargo.
- June 7, 1979: Purchased by the Seattle Mariners from the St. Louis Cardinals.

A first round draft pick of the Giants in 1972, Dressler was a disappointment to Bay Area fans in 1976, struggling to a 3-10 record. His stay with the Cardinals was very short, three games (including two starts) in September 1978, a 0-1 record in 13 innings.

He wound up his career in his native Northwest (he is from Portland, Oregon) with poor Mariners' teams in 1979 & 1980, compiling a 7-12 record before being released early in 1981.

Rob is now Vice President and CEO of Oregon Roses, Inc. a floral supplier of wreaths and fresh cut flowers, a business he has been involved in since 1992.

Taylor Duncan

- September 7, 1977: Selected off waivers by the St. Louis Cardinals from the Baltimore Orioles.
- December 5, 1977: Drafted by the Oakland Athletics from the St. Louis Cardinals in the 1977 rule 5 draft.

A first round draft pick of the Braves in 1971, Duncan made his major league debut with the Cardinals in September 1977. Taylor batted .333 in 12 at bats with the club, clubbing his first major league homer that month against the Mets. Drafted by the A's off the Cardinals minor league roster, Taylor played one more season in the bigs, hitting .257 with 37 RBI's in 1978.

Taylor toiled in the minors until 1983, including a season in Japan and three years in the Mexican League. He died in January 2004 from complications of a stroke.

Don Durham

- June 4, 1970: Drafted by the St. Louis Cardinals in the 7th round of the 1970 amateur draft.
- July 16, 1973: Traded by the St. Louis Cardinals to the Texas Rangers for Jim Kremmel.

Durham, promoted from the minors in July 1972 as a starter, was known more for his bat than his arm. Batting .500 with the Cardinals in 1972 with 2 home runs did not make up for his 2-7 record and 4.34 ERA on the mound. His major league career ended the following season with Texas with a career mark of 2-11 with a 5.83 ERA. Durham ended up in Nashville Tennessee operating an automobile body repair shop.

Jim Dwyer

- June 8, 1971: Drafted by the St. Louis Cardinals in the 11th round of the 1971 amateur draft. Player signed June 19, 1971.
- July 25, 1975: Traded by the St. Louis Cardinals to the Montreal Expos for Larry Lintz.
- September 13, 1977: Signed as a Free Agent with the St. Louis Cardinals.
- June 15, 1978: the St. Louis Cardinals sent Jim Dwyer to the San Francisco Giants to complete an earlier deal made on October 25, 1977.

A dependable pinch-hitter and part-time outfielder/first baseman, Dwyer could not duplicate the success he attained in the minor leagues. A two-time American Association batting leader, Jim hit a solid .260 over 18 years in the majors. His best season as a Cardinal was 1974 when he batted .279 in limited duty. A key man off the bench during the 1983 Baltimore Orioles World Series title, Dwyer is currently 17th among all-time major league leaders in pinch hits with 103.

After his retirement as a player, Dwyer has stayed in the game as a manager/hitting coach/coordinator; the past 17 years in the Twins organization. He is currently hitting coach for the Twins Fort Myers minor league team.

Rawly Eastwick

- June 15, 1977: Traded by the Cincinnati Reds to the St. Louis Cardinals for Doug Capilla.
- November 2, 1977: Granted Free Agency.

Acquired at the trading deadline, Eastwick had a rough go with the Redbirds in 1977, ending with a 3-7 record, 4.70 ERA and 74 hits allowed in 53 2/3 innings. It was quite a change from the previous two seasons, where Rawly lead the league in saves in both 1975 & '76 earning World Series rings, with 22 and 26 respectively. Eastwick was especially effective in the classic 1975 World Series against the Red Sox, winning games 2 and 3, and saving game 5.

Rawly signed with the Yankees for big money after the 1977 season, but had few opportunities behind stellar relievers Rich Gossage and Sparky Lyle. His career ended in 1981 after eight seasons, a 28-27 record, 3.31 ERA and 68 career saves.

An accomplished artist and antique collector, Rawly lives in the Boston area of all places, where he is involved in office building ownership and management.

Ron Fairly

- December 6, 1974: Traded by the Montreal Expos to the St. Louis Cardinals for Ed Kurpiel (minors) and Rudy Kinard (minors).
- September 14, 1976: Purchased by the Oakland Athletics from the St. Louis Cardinals.

Ron Fairly's name has been associated with baseball for 48 years, 21 as a player and 27 after his career ended in 1978. He was a valuable utility and spot starter both seasons with the Redbirds, especially in 1975 where he batted .301, (his best average since 1961) with 7 homers and 37 RBI's. A first baseman/outfielder, Fairly won three World Series titles, all with the Dodgers in 1959, '63, and '65. A member of the 1977 expansion Blue Jays, Ron has the unique status of representing both Canadian clubs in All Star games ('69 with Montreal, '77 with Toronto.) His career ended with a .266 average and close to 2000 runs batted in.

Ron moved into broadcasting, mostly as a color man, for the Angels, Giants and Mariners between 1979 and 2006, when Ron announced his retirement.

Pete Falcone

- December 8, 1975: Traded by the San Francisco Giants to the St. Louis Cardinals for Ken Reitz.
- December 5, 1978: Traded by the St. Louis Cardinals to the New York Mets for Tom Grieve and Kim Seaman.

A hard-throwing lefty, Falcone was second on the staff with 12 wins in 1976, though he had 16 losses. He never had a season with double digit victories again. After a poor start in 1977, Falcone was sent to the bullpen and eventually, the minor leagues for a while, winning only 4 games that season. Pete seemed to lose focus and concentration after giving up a walk or home run.

1978 was no better, starting 0-5 before finishing with a 2-7 record and 5.76 ERA. He was sent to his native New York after the season, where he experienced limited success. Pete was "just tired of baseball" by the time he retired from Atlanta in 1984 with a career 70-90 record and 4.07 ERA.

In 1995, Pete was named manager in the Texas-Louisiana league where he was employed through 1999. He currently has a catering business in the Alexandria, Louisiana area.

Bobby Fenwick

- November 28, 1972: Traded by the Houston Astros with Ray Busse to the St. Louis Cardinals for Skip Jutze and Milt Ramirez.
- June 12, 1973: Released by the St. Louis Cardinals.

Bobby, the 2nd major leaguer of Japanese ancestry (Mike Lum being the first) made the 1973 opening day roster as a reserve infielder. He had only 6 at bats and 1 hit before being released by the team in June of that year. He finished his major league career with ten hits. After his career ended the following year in the minors, Fenwick moved back to his native Minnesota. He's been involved in local government for a number of years, as well as manager of a forest products company. One of his fondest memories of the bigs was his locker nesting between Joe Torre and Tim McCarver.

Joe Ferguson

- June 15, 1976: Traded by the Los Angeles Dodgers with Fred Tisdale (minors) and Bob Detherage to the St. Louis Cardinals for Reggie Smith.
- November 23, 1976: Traded by the St. Louis Cardinals with Bob Detherage to the Houston Astros for Jerry DaVanon and Larry Dierker.

A Dodger for 11 of his 14 major league seasons, Ferguson was acquired at the 1976 trading deadline because the team had doubts about being able to sign Reggie Smith. The plan was for Ferguson to replace Simmons at catcher and Simmons to move to first base. Joe, who had a stellar year with the Dodgers in 1973, batting .263 with 25 homers and 88 RBI's, did not respond this time, batting only .201 with 21 RBI's. He was traded after the season.

Upon his retirement in 1983 with a career .240 average, Joe remained in the game, first as a major league coach with Texas (1986-87), the Dodgers (1988 /89 & 1992 & '93), and a coach in the minor leagues for 15+ years in the Dodgers, Orioles and Padres organization.

Mike Fiore

- March 20, 1972: Traded by the Boston Red Sox to the St. Louis Cardinals for Bob Burda.
- June 20, 1972: Traded by the St. Louis Cardinals with Bob Chlupsa to the San Diego Padres for Rafael Robles. Mike Fiore returned to original team on July 3, 1972.

Mike, appearing in 254 games during his 5-year big league career, had only 10 at bats for the Cardinals in 1972 with 1 hit- that 1 hit a game-winner against the Braves. A .274 hitter in 107 games with the expansion Royals in 1969, Fiore hit the first home run in Royals history against the A's.

After Mikes' major league career , he proceeded to play in the minors through the 1978 season. His son Mike earned a gold metal in the 1988 Olympics for the U.S. baseball team and was later drafted by the Cardinals.

Eddie Fisher

- August 29, 1973: Purchased by the St. Louis Cardinals from the Chicago White Sox.
- October 26, 1973: Released by the St. Louis Cardinals.

Fisher, acquired for the 1973 stretch run had a 2-1 record and 1.29 ERA for the Cardinals. With the glut of relievers in the bullpen, the 36-year old Fisher was released shortly thereafter.

One of the first of the late-inning relievers, the knuckleballer led the A.L. in appearances in 1965 & 66, winning a World Series with the other Birds (Baltimore) in 1966. Eddie finished his 15 year career with a 85-70 record, 3.41 ERA with 81 saves.

Fisher retired after the '73 season and returned to his longtime home in Oklahoma, where he began a career in the insurance business. He was inducted into the Oklahoma Sports Hall of Fame in 2008.

Rich Folkers

- October 18, 1971: Traded by the New York Mets with Jim Bibby, Charlie Hudson and Art Shamsky to the St. Louis Cardinals for Jim Beauchamp, Chip Coulter, Harry Parker and Chuck Taylor.
- November 18, 1974: Traded by the St. Louis Cardinals with Alan Foster and Sonny Siebert to the San Diego Padres for a player to be named later and Ed Brinkman. The San Diego Padres sent Danny Breeden (December 10, 1974) to the
- St. Louis Cardinals to complete the trade.

Rich enjoyed an 11-6 record during his three-year tenure with the club from 72-74. Typically used in middle relief against left-handed lineups, Rich had a great season in his final one with the team in 1974, posting a 6-2 record with a 3.00 ERA.

That was a great baseball town," said Folkers. "They always had a great crowd there. The thing about St. Louis was the fans are very knowledgeable. They know good play. Even if it's the visiting club, they appreciate good baseball. It was quite an experience." Known for the famous malaprop from Padres announcer Jerry Coleman, "Folkers is now throwing up in the bullpen", Rich ended his career in 1977 with a seven year mark of 19-23, 4.11 ERA, later becoming a coach at Eckerd College in Florida.

Bob Forsch

- June 7, 1968: Drafted by the St. Louis Cardinals in the 26th round of the 1968 amateur draft.
- November 12, 1986: Granted Free Agency.
- December 19, 1986: Signed as a Free Agent with the St. Louis Cardinals.
- December 21, 1987: Released by the St. Louis Cardinals.

- January 27, 1988: Signed as a Free Agent with the St. Louis Cardinals.
- August 31, 1988: Traded by the St. Louis Cardinals to the Houston Astros for Denny Walling.

BOB FORSCH — PITCHER

A Cardinal for fifteen of his sixteen major league seasons, Forsch was a well-liked, competitive pitcher who won 163 games with the club.

I remember his inaugural start at Riverfront Stadium against the Reds in 1974, with the hope that his contributions could lead the team to a division title. Not that season, but Forsch accomplished a great deal: namely two no hitters in 1978 & 83 along with his brother Ken, the only brothers to both twirl no hitters; a 20 game winner in 1977; winningest pitcher in old Busch Stadium (1966-2005) with 93 victories; third amongst Cardinal pitchers of all time with 163 wins, not to mention two Silver Slugger Awards as the leagues best hitting pitcher in 1980 & 1987. Forsch finally gained a division title in the 1980's, winning a World Series ring in 1982.

After closing out his career with Houston in 1989, Forsch later was pitching coach in the Reds minor league affiliate for three seasons. In October 2011, Bob threw out the first pitch for game seven in the epic World Series between the Cards and Texas. He passed away less than a week later from an aneurysm at 61.

Alan Foster

- April 5, 1973: Purchased by the St. Louis Cardinals from the California Angels.
- November 18, 1974: Traded by the St. Louis Cardinals with Rich Folkers and Sonny Siebert to the San Diego Padres for a

player to be named later and Ed Brinkman. The San Diego Padres sent Danny Breeden (December 10, 1974) to the St. Louis Cardinals to complete the trade.

The Cardinals biggest pitching surprise of 1973, Foster made the club as a non-roster player in spring training. After a rugged 0-3 start (the team was 5-20 at the start of the season) Alan finished with a 13-9 record, 3.14 ERA and 2 of his 6 career shutouts. After inking a huge signing bonus with the Dodgers in 1965, Foster proceeded to pitch 2 no-hitters in the minor leagues in 1967. His fastball was never the same after injuring his arm the following season; he gained more notoriety by giving up the first home run hit out of Dodger Stadium (Willie Stargell, 1969). During the offseason Foster was part of a guitar and song act with former teammate Tommy Hutton, as well as selling real estate, but baseball was his true love.

Foster was eventually dropped from the Redbirds rotation in September 1974, finishing up his career in San Diego in 1976, where he still makes his home. He left with a 48-63 record over a decade in the game.

George Frazier

- December 8, 1977: Traded by the Milwaukee Brewers to the St. Louis Cardinals for Buck Martinez.
- June 7, 1981: the St. Louis Cardinals sent George Frazier to the New York Yankees to complete an earlier deal made on February 16, 1981.
- February 16, 1981: The St. Louis Cardinals sent a player to be named later to the New York Yankees for Rafael Santana.

A middle reliever most of his career Frazier, a Springfield, Missouri native, began his 10-year career with the Redbirds in 1978. The sinkerball pitcher was a cumulative 3-11 with a 3.84 ERA between 1978 and 1980, his best season being 1980, with 3 saves and a 2.74 ERA.

Acquired by the Yankees, George had his best season in 1981 with a 1.63 ERA and three saves. In the World Series that year, Frazier tied the record of most losses by a pitcher in a World Series, with three, losing Games 3, 4, and 6. Frazier was touched by Yankees owner George Steinbrenner's kind words after the series, as well as flying George and his family on his private jet back to Springfield when his father suffered a stroke.

George last pitched in the majors in 1987, winning a World Series ring with Minnesota's victory over the Cardinals.

A baseball broadcaster since 1988, George is in his 16th season as color analyst for the Colorado Rockies.

Roger Freed

- December 6, 1976: Drafted by the St. Louis Cardinals from the Montreal Expos in the 1976 rule 5 draft.
- April 2, 1980: Released by the St. Louis Cardinals.

A cult hero amongst Cardinal fans in 1977. Freed was clutch off the bench, toying with the .400 mark until the last game of the season. Roger, International League MVP in 1970, hit the first grand slam in the Phillies Veterans Stadium history in 1971, but it would not be his last. Roger, a utility player, had his greatest season with the Birds in '77, hitting .398 with 5 homers and 21 RBI's. He dropped off significantly the following two seasons, to .239 and .258 in '78 & '79, his last major league duty. However, in his last season Roger blasted a game winning, walk-off grand slam against the Astros Joe Sambito (I was there), one of only 25 in major league history (and joining the Redbirds Carl Taylor in 1970).

Freed later managed a season in the Cardinals minor league in 1981 and the Mexican League in 1985. Suffering a ruptured appendix in December 1995, Freed died of heart-related issued in January 1996 at the age of 49.

Dan Frisella

- April 8, 1976: Traded by the San Diego Padres to the St. Louis Cardinals for Bob Stewart (minors) and Ken Reynolds.
- June 7, 1976: Traded by the St. Louis Cardinals to the Milwaukee Brewers for a player to be named later. The Milwaukee Brewers sent Sam Mejias (June 23, 1976) to the St. Louis Cardinals to complete the trade.

Frisella was a Redbird for only two months in 1976, appearing in 18 games with a 3.97 ERA and one save. His greatest success had been with the Mets in 1970 & 1971, where he earned 8 victories each season and had 12 saves with a 1.99 ERA in '71. Upon his trade from the Redbirds, Dan had a resurgence in his career winning 5 and saving 9 with a 2.74 ERA for the Brewers in 1976.

Tragically, Dan was killed New Year's Day 1977 when he was crushed in a dune buggy accident at the age of 30.

John Fulgham

- June 8, 1976: Drafted by the St. Louis Cardinals in the 1st round (15th pick) of the 1976 amateur draft (June Secondary).

A local Pattonville High School grad, Fulgham made his major league pitching debut a great one, twirling a complete game shutout. His 1979 season ended with a solid 10-6 record, 2.53 ERA and 2 shutouts, all of his victories being complete games. Shoulder injuries, later to be diagnosed as a rotator cuff injury, limited his 1980 season to a 4-6 record. Once again, all of his four victories were complete game victories. Fulgham never made it back to the majors, ending his professional career in 1983.

Fulgham later coached in the college ranks, including Rollins College in Florida, before earning his BS and MBA. He worked for twenty years as a financial consultant and advisor until 2004, when he became senior vice president of investment management at Rochdale Investment Management in Florida.

Phil Gagliano

- September 6, 1959: Signed by the St. Louis Cardinals as an amateur free agent.
- May 29, 1970: Traded by the St. Louis Cardinals to the Chicago Cubs for Ted Abernathy.

Gagliano, who enjoyed an eight year career with the Redbirds (and 2 World Series rings) was primarily a backup infielder before being traded to the Reds. A career .238 hitter in twelve big league seasons, 1965 was his only season where he batted more than 300 times, compiling a .240 average with 8 homers and 53 ribbies.

Upon his retirement in 1974, Gagliano became a scout for the Cardinals in the St. Louis area.

Mike Garman

- December 7, 1973: Traded by the Boston Red Sox with John Curtis and Lynn McGlothen to the St. Louis Cardinals for Reggie Cleveland, Terry Hughes and Diego Segui.
- October 28, 1975: Traded by the St. Louis Cardinals with a player to be named later to the Chicago Cubs for Don Kessinger. The St. Louis Cardinals sent Bobby Hrapmann (minors) (April 5, 1976) to the Chicago Cubs to complete the trade.

The first first-round pick from Idaho in baseball history, Garman enjoyed two good years with the Cardinals in 1974 & 75. Along with lefty Hrabosky, Garman was the right-hander out of the pen those two seasons, accumulating 16 saves and a 2.52 ERA. A couple of wild throws to first and third base in 1975 dropped his record to 3-8 that season before being dispatched to the Cubs after the season.

Mike had back-to-back thirteen save seasons in 1977 and '78 but irritated Montreal management when he refused to be inserted into a game due to overwork. His major league career ended upon the conclusion of the season at 22-27 overall and 42 saves. Garman moved back to Idaho after that, working with his brother farming orchards and corn. He later became an insurance broker with Farm Bureau Insurance, where former big leaguer Bill Buckner is a client.

Wayne Garrett

- July 21, 1978: Purchased by the <u>St. Louis Cardinals</u> from the <u>Montreal Expos</u>.

Part of the "Miracle Mets" of 1969, Wayne was a steady performer with a good glove during his ten year career, eight of them with the Mets. His best season was 1973, where Wayne batted .256 with 16 homers and 58 RBI's, leading the National League champs in game winning hits with 11. By 1978, St. Louis was the last stop in his career where he ended on a high note, batting 333 in 63 at bats with a homer and 10 runs batted in.

The Cardinals and Garrett could not agree on a contract for the following season, so Wayne finished out his career with two seasons in Japan along with his brother Adrian, an eight year major league veteran himself. He left with a career .239 average.

After baseball, Wayne was involved in sales for his older brother's irrigation company as well as work with a courier business in Sarasota, Florida, where he makes his home.

Bob Gibson

- Before 1957 Season: Signed by the <u>St. Louis Cardinals</u> as an amateur free agent.

"He's the luckiest pitcher I ever saw. He always pitches when the other team doesn't score any runs." - Tim McCarver

My all-time personal baseball hero, Gibby was still an intimidating presence in 1970, earning yet another Cy Young Award for his 23-7 record as well as a no-hitter in 1971. After a very good 19-11 record in 1972, age and injuries began to take its toll. Bob retired late in the 1975 season: "When I gave up a grand slam to Pete LaCock, I knew it was time to quit." He ended his career with 251 wins, 5-20 win seasons, the 1968 MVP AND Cy Young Award, along with 9 Gold Gloves.

Upon his retirement from the game and his induction into the Hall of Fame (1981), Gibson followed his battery mate and manager Joe Torre as pitching coach to the Mets (1981), Braves (1982-84) and Cardinals (1995). Bob is also a board member of the Baseball Assistance Team, which assists ex-players through times of medical or financial hardship.

Danny Godby

- December 14, 1971: Traded by the <u>Cincinnati Reds</u> to the <u>St. Louis Cardinals</u> for <u>Carroll Sembera</u>.
- March 29, 1975: Traded by the <u>St. Louis Cardinals</u> to the <u>Boston Red Sox</u> for <u>Danny Cater</u>.

Godby saw his only major league action in 1974 with the Cardinals, batting .154 in 13 at bats with 1 RBI. In his first game, Danny singled and scored the winning run against San Diego. He also played in the 25 inning marathon against the Mets, going 0 for 2. He felt he might have a chance with the Red Sox if their two rookies did not work out in Boston the following season. However, the two rookies were guys named Rice and Lynn. His career ended after 1977.

Godby, who earned a degree at Bowling Green State, returned to his native West Virginia and taught for over forty years. Still involved in athletics, Danny was assistant and head coach in basketball, winning over 250 games. He assisted with baseball as well. He has also been involved in his community, having served as county commissioner for over twenty years until 2010.

Wayne Granger

- Before 1965 Season: Signed by the St. Louis Cardinals as an amateur free agent.
- October 11, 1968: Traded by the St. Louis Cardinals with Bobby Tolan to the Cincinnati Reds for Vada Pinson.
- November 29, 1972: Traded by the Minnesota Twins to the St. Louis Cardinals for John Cumberland and Larry Hisle.
- August 7, 1973: Traded by the St. Louis Cardinals to the New York Yankees for a player to be named later and cash. The New York Yankees sent Ken Crosby (September 12, 1973) to the St. Louis Cardinals to complete the trade.

A 6'4" spindly sinkerball pitcher, Granger saw work for the Redbirds in 1968, appearing in 34 games with a solid 4-2 record and 2.25 ERA. His career really took off after his trade to Cincinnati. National League Fireman of the Year in 1969 & 1970, Granger lead the league in games in 1969 & 1971 and saves in 1970 with 35.

After a spotty season in Minnesota, Wayne was reacquired by the Cardinals at the conclusion of the 1972 season. Wayne's 1973 season was inconsistent, with a 2-4 record and 4.24 ERA and 5 saves. His career ended at the end of the 70's with appearances in the Mexican and AAA leagues, ending with 108 major league saves. A member of the Cincinnati Reds Hall of Fame (1982), Wayne still appears at "Redsfest" fan events.

Bill Greif

- May 19, 1976: Traded by the San Diego Padres to the St. Louis Cardinals for Luis Melendez.
- November 6, 1976: Traded by the St. Louis Cardinals with Sam Mejias and Angel Torres to the Montreal Expos for Steve Dunning, Pat Scanlon and Tony Scott.

A starter for the 1972-1974 Padres, Greif had a abysmal 24-52 record during those years for some equally abysimal teams. Long coveted by the Cardinals, Greif was inserted as a setup man for closer Al Hrabosky. After a promising start with the club, his fortunes tumbled much as the team did in 1976. He finished his season with the Redbirds with a 1-5 record, 4.12 ERA and six saves. He played one more year in baseball, 1978 in the minors, ending his six-year career with a career 31-67 record.

Bill has enjoyed a successful career in real estate in Texas, including real estate investments. He is also co-founder of Cancer Connection, an organization that offers support and encouragement to families with cancer.

Tom Grieve

- December 5, 1978: Traded by the New York Mets with Kim Seaman to the St. Louis Cardinals for Pete Falcone.
- May 9, 1979: Released by the St. Louis Cardinals.

At the end of his nine-year career, Grieve was three for fifteen in nine games with the Cards in 1979. The Cards felt Roger Freed was a better pinch-hitter, so Grieve was released, never to appear in another professional game. Originally a first round pick of the Washington Senators in 1966, Tom had his best season with the transplanted Rangers in 1976, hitting .255 with 20 homers and 81 RBI's. His cumulative average for his career was .249.

After retiring from professional baseball, Tom moved into broadcasting as the Rangers color man in 1980. In 1984, Tom was appointed general manager of the Rangers, a position he held until 1994. After his run ended, he moved back into broadcasting to this day, ultimately working for the Washington/Texas franchise in 45 of his 46 years in baseball. A member of the Rangers Hall of Fame (2010), Toms' son Ben was a major leaguer for nine seasons. Tom and Ben are the first father and son duo to both be number one draft picks.

Mario Guerrero

- April 4, 1975: Traded by the Boston Red Sox to the St. Louis Cardinals for a player to be named later. The St. Louis Cardinals sent Jim Willoughby (July 4, 1975) to the Boston Red Sox to complete the trade.
- May 29, 1976: Traded by the St. Louis Cardinals to the California Angels for a player to be named later and Ed Jordan (minors). The California Angels sent Ed Kurpiel (minors) (July 30, 1976) to the St. Louis Cardinals to complete the trade.

Guerrero had success as a part-time shortstop, putting together three consecutive .275 + seasons from 1976-'78. When the slick fielder had a full time position with the 1978 A's, he batted a respectable .275 with 38 RBI's. He did not get much of an opportunity with the Cardinals in 1975, batting .239 in 64 games, and never appeared with the club again. His major league tenure petered out by 1980 with a .257 career average.

Guerrero later gained notoriety becoming a "buscone", or talent hunter of young baseball players in his native Dominican Republic. He sued a number of players, including Raul Mondesi and Geronimo Berroa, claiming he was owed future earnings based on his advice.

Joe Grzenda

- November 3, 1971: Traded by the Texas Rangers to the St. Louis Cardinals for Ted Kubiak.

Joe, 35 years old and in the last of his 8-year career, pitched in 30 games with the Redbirds in 1972, with a 1-0 record and 5.66 ERA. His career ended with 14 victories and 14 saves. His claim to fame was being the last Washington Senators pitcher on the mound in their final game in 1971. Because fans stormed the field before the last out, the game was forfeited. Joe still has the ball from that appearance! Upon his retirement from the game, Grzenda moved back to Northeastern Pennsylvania and became a security guard, then later worked at a battery factory for 25 years. Enjoying retirement, Joe walks up to 3 1/2 miles each day.

Santiago Guzman

- Before 1967 Season: Signed by the St. Louis Cardinals as an amateur free agent.

A early 1970's hurler, who I thought would dominate, Guzman never lived up to his billing as the next Bob Gibson due to arm problems. He earned his only major league victory in 1970 (against 2 losses) with a complete game 5-hitter against Houston. Arm problems began to plague Santiago in 1971, despite the fact he struck out 10 Mets in one start and compiled ten unearned innings that season. His seven year professional career ended in 1973 in the Class A league with a 62-35 record, 3.07 ERA in the minors. He then retired to his home in the Dominican Republic.

Joe Hague

- Before 1966 Season: Signed by the St. Louis Cardinals as an amateur free agent.
- May 19, 1972: Traded by the St. Louis Cardinals to the Cincinnati Reds for Bernie Carbo.

A two-sport athlete at the University of Texas, Joe began his five- year career with the Redbirds in 1968. A starting first baseman in 1970 and 1971, his best season was 1970 with a .271 average, 14 home runs and 68 RBI's. After becoming frustrated with Cardinal ownership in 1972 (see Carlton, Steve; Reuss, Jerry) Joe was shipped off to Cincinnati where he appeared in the World Series that season. After leaving the Reds the following season, Joe bounced around the minor and Mexican leagues. His six-year major league career ended with a .239 batting average. Sadly, Joe passed away in 1994 at the too young age of 50.

Don Hahn

- May 21, 1975: Signed as a Free Agent with the St. Louis Cardinals.
- June 24, 1975: Purchased by the San Diego Padres from the St. Louis Cardinals.

A poor hitting, good fielding centerfielder, Hahn appeared in only seven games with the Cards in 1975, with one hit in eight at bats. Hahn had the distinction of starting the inaugural game in Montreal Expos history in 1969 and hitting the first inside the park home run in

Philadelphia's Veteran's Stadium. Replacing the retired Willie Mays in 1974 for the Mets, Hahn played in a career high 110 games for the Mets, batting .251.

Hahn ended his seven year major league career career in 1975, with a .236 average. He moved into a real estate career in the San Francisco area, where he still resides. Hahn enjoys hunting and fishing in his spare time.

Dave Hamilton

- June 15, 1975: Traded by the Oakland Athletics with Chet Lemon to the Chicago White Sox for Stan Bahnsen and Skip Pitlock.
- November 28, 1977: the Chicago White Sox sent Dave Hamilton and Silvio Martinez to the St. Louis Cardinals to complete an earlier deal made on August 31, 1977.
- August 31, 1977: The Chicago White Sox sent players to be named later to the St. Louis Cardinals for Clay Carroll.
- May 28, 1978: Purchased by the Pittsburgh Pirates from the St. Louis Cardinals.

Winner of World Series rings his first three seasons in the bigs, (though appearing in only the 1972 Series) Hamilton was the fifth starter for the "Swinging A's from 1972-1974. Never a double digit winner, Hamilton had his best season in 1974, where he had a 7-4 record and 3.15 ERA. The lefthander appeared in only 13 games (all losses) with the Redbirds in 1978, after which manager Vern Rapp quickly lost patience with him. After allowing 4 homers in 5 1/3 innings, Hamilton was dealt to Pittsburgh after a Cardinals career of 0-0, 6.43 ERA in 14 innings. He ended his career in 1980 back in Oakland with a career mark of 39-41 and 3.85 ERA.

Now a high school baseball coach in San Ramon, California since 1996, Dave is also a project manager for a roofing contractor.

Larry Haney

- September 1, 1973: Purchased with Lew Krausse by the St. Louis Cardinals from the Oakland Athletics.
- March 26, 1974: Purchased by the Oakland Athletics from the St. Louis Cardinals.

Haney had the proverbial "cup of coffee" with the Cardinals in September 1973, catching 4 innings over 2 games with 1 hitless at bat.
A twelve -year defensive catcher, Larry batted .215 with a number of teams, including 3 different runs with the Oakland A's. Owner of 3 World Series rings (1966, 1972 & 74), Haney was the last of the original Seattle Pilots to wear the Brewers uniform in the final game of his career in 1978.

Upon retirement as a player, Haney enjoyed over 28 years in the Brewers organization, including stints as bullpen coach (1978-1989) and pitching coach (1990-91). His son Chris was a major league pitcher in the 90's, mainly with Kansas City.

Vic Harris

- December 22, 1975: Traded by the Chicago Cubs to the St. Louis Cardinals for Mick Kelleher.
- October 20, 1976: Traded by the St. Louis Cardinals with Willie Crawford and John Curtis to the San Francisco Giants for Mike Caldwell, John D'Acquisto and Dave Rader.

May of 1976 was the highlight of Vic Harris' time with the Cardinals. Filling in at second base for an injured Mike Tyson, Harris was named N.L. Player of the Week for his 7 RBI's (he had 19 total for the season). His performance tapered off as the season went on, much as the teams' did as well. He ended up batting .228 in 282 at bats, a little better than his career .217 mark.

A starter for only one of his eight seasons, (1973 with Texas), Harris batted .249 with 8 homers and 44 RBI's that season. After three seasons in Japan and a final season in AAA Louisville, Harris called it quits in 1984.

Chuck Hartenstein

- June 22, 1970: Selected off waivers by the St. Louis Cardinals from the Pittsburgh Pirates.
- July 14, 1970: Sent to the Boston Red Sox by the St. Louis Cardinals as part of a conditional deal

1970-13 1/3 Innings, 24 hits, 13 earned runs, 8.78 ERA, such was the state of the Cardinals bullpen in 1970. Chuck had an unusual path back to the majors after leaving Boston at the conclusion of the '70 season. It was another seven years before Hartenstein appeared in another major league game, with the Toronto Blue Jays in 1977. He finished his six-year career 17-19, 4.52 ERA and 23 saves.

Following his major league career, Chuck coached for the Cleveland Indians and Milwaukee Brewers. A star pitcher with the Texas Longhorns, Chuck was inducted into the Longhorns Hall of Fame in 2004

Jack Heidemann

- June 1, 1974: Traded by the Cleveland Indians to the St. Louis Cardinals for Luis Alvarado and Ed Crosby.
- December 11, 1974: Traded by the St. Louis Cardinals with Mike Vail to the New York Mets for Ted Martinez.

With Mike Tyson struggling at shortstop in 1974, the Cardinals traded Luis Alvarado for Heidemann, a former number one pick of Cleveland in 1967. Jack batted .271, a career high for the team with three ribbies in seventy at bats. A career .211 hitter over eight seasons, Jack was traded at the end of the season, another in the revolving door of post-Dal Maxvill shortstops; Ramirez, Anderson, Kubiak, Busse.

Now living in the Phoenix area, Jack has been a realtor for over thirty years serving the area. For the past twenty years Jack still puts on the uniform for the area Baseball Charities Celebrity Game which benefits little league teams throughout the state of Arizona

Tom Heintzelman

- June 7, 1968: Drafted by the St. Louis Cardinals in the 7th round of the 1968 amateur draft.
- October 14, 1974: Traded by the St. Louis Cardinals to the San Francisco Giants for Jim Willoughby.

A St. Charles Missouri native, Heintzelman was a good fielding infielder in 61 games during the 1973 & 74 seasons with the Redbirds. He enjoyed a .310 average in 29 at bats for the club in 1973 but could not duplicate his numbers the following year. After a very brief stop in San Francisco in '77 & 78, his major league career ended with a .243 average and 34 major league hits. Tom now enjoys hunting, fishing, golf and especially, his nine grandchildren. His father Ken was a major league pitcher from 1937-1952 with the Pirates and Phillies.

Bob Heise

- December 8, 1973: Traded by the Milwaukee Brewers to the St. Louis Cardinals for Tom Murphy.
- July 31, 1974: Traded by the St. Louis Cardinals to the California Angels for a player to be named later. The California Angels sent Doug Howard (October 7, 1974) to the St. Louis Cardinals to complete the trade.

Heise, brought up to the club due to a Ted Sizemore injury, appeared in only three games, going 1 for 7. A career utilityman, Heise lasted parts of eleven seasons in the majors, batting .247 overall. In 1975, he knocked in 21 runs off the bench in earning an A.L. Champion ring for the Red Sox. His eleven-year career ended after the 1977 season with only one season of more than 200 at bats.

Bob became a police and corrections officer for 26 years. One of the venues he worked was the famous (or infamous) San Quentin Prison. He also fought fires for 16 years. A cancer survivor after a two and a half years fight, Bob now enjoys retirement, playing golf a couple times a week.

George Hendrick

- May 26, 1978: Traded by the San Diego Padres to the St. Louis Cardinals for Eric Rasmussen.
- December 12, 1984: Traded by the St. Louis Cardinals with Steve Barnard (minors) to the Pittsburgh Pirates for Brian Harper and John Tudor.

"Silent George" known for his non-communication with the press, was a key acquisition in the Cardinals climb back to the World Series in 1982. His departure in 1984 for future ace John Tudor extended the Whitey Ball era a few more seasons. A four-time All Star (1974, 1975, 1980, 1983), Silver Slugger in 1980 and 1983, George won series rings in 1972 with the A's and the 1982 Cards, hitting .321 in the series against Milwaukee. Hendrick enjoyed three .300+ seasons with the Cardinals as well as two 100+ RBI years. Late in the 1979 season George established a trend that still holds true today; he is the first player to wear his uniform pants all the way down to his shoe tops. Garry Templeton followed him shortly thereafter and soon, the league as well. He batted a solid .294 in seven seasons with the Cardinals. His 18- year major league run ended in 1988 with an overall .278 average and over 1100 RBI's.

George worked in the Cardinal organization from 1993-1997 as a minor league hitting and outfield instructor and hitting coach for the Cardinals in 1996 and '97. After a seven year run as an instructor in the Angels and Dodgers organization, George accepted the position as firstbase/outfield coach for Tampa Bay in 2005, a position he still holds today.

Keith Hernandez

- June 8, 1971: Drafted by the St. Louis Cardinals in the 42nd round of the 1971 amateur draft.
- June 15, 1983: Traded by the St. Louis Cardinals to the New York Mets for Neil Allen and Rick Ownbey.

After two great seasons in AAA Tulsa, Keith Hernandez was ready to supplant Joe Torre at first base for the team in 1975. After an early struggle that season and a return to the minors, Keith never looked back, enjoying a 17-year career in the majors.

A great fielding first baseman, Hernandez won 11 consecutive Gold Gloves, the most of any first baseman. Winner of the 1979 bat-

KEITH HERNANDEZ   FIRST BASEMAN

ting title (.344) and co-MVP (with Willie Stargell), Keith batted over .300 seven times in his storied career.

After winning the first of his two World Series rings in 1982, manager Whitey Herzog traded Keith to the Mets in 1983, disappointed with Keith's lazy work habits, poor attitude, and possible substance abuse. Keith, later in his career, agreed with Whitey's assessment of his career at that point. Hernandez was big in New York, helping the Mets to their second ever World Series title in 1986 and a constant source of derision by Cardinal fans. He finished with a career .296 mark and over 2000 hits.

Keith still embraces the bright lights of New York where he currently is an analyst on the Mets network. He has written four books, appeared on an episode of the television show Seinfeld, and appeared on a advertisement with Walt "Clyde" Frazier for a hair coloring commercial, Just for Men.

Larry Herndon

- June 8, 1971: Drafted by the St. Louis Cardinals in the 3rd round of the 1971 amateur draft.
- May 9, 1975: Traded by the St. Louis Cardinals with Luis Gonzalez (minors) to the San Francisco Giants for Ron Bryant.

Herndon appeared in only twelve games in September 1974, primarily as a pinch runner. In his only at bat with the Cardinals, Larry singled. His greatest fame with the Cardinal organization was rooming with Randall Poffo in the minor leagues. Poffo would soon leave baseball and become wrestler "Macho Man" Randy Savage.

His 14-year career would prosper in San Francisco and later, Detroit. Larry's best seasons were with the Tigers, where he batted .292 with 23 homers and 88 ribbies in 1982 and .302, 20 and 92 in 1983. Larrys' home run in Game One of the 1984 World Series gave the Tigers the lead they would not relinquish. He also caught the last out of the series, giving the Tigers their first World Championship since, well, 1968 against the Redbirds. Larry enjoyed a fine career, batting a solid .274.

A hitting coach from 1992-1998 for the Tigers, Larry has worked in the Class A Lakeland Tigers organization since 2005.

Tom Herr

- August 22, 1974: Signed by the St. Louis Cardinals as an amateur free agent.
- April 22, 1988: Traded by the St. Louis Cardinals to the Minnesota Twins for Tom Brunansky.

A key contributor to the Redbirds teams of the '80's, Tom enjoyed 10 of his 13 major league seasons with the team starting in 1979. After earning his World Series ring in 1982, Tom was shut down for much of the 1983 season with surgery to both of his knees. He came back after a solid 1984 season to experience a career-year in 1985, where he batted .302 with 110 RBI's, including an All-Star appearance. His 8 home runs that season is the current National League record for most ribbies with under ten home runs. One of the biggest thrills of a great 1987 season was Tommy's walk-off grand slam home run against the hated Mets during seat cushion night. Cushions rained down on the field. I kept mine however, until age and an expanding waistline destroyed the remnants of that evening! In 1988 with the N.L. champs in a slump (shut out four times in 10 games) and with departed Jack Clark no longer batting behind him, Herr was traded to the World Champion Twins. He played with three more teams before calling it quits after 1991 with a career .271 average, 1450 hits and 188 stolen bases.

Beginning in 2004, Herr managed and coached for his native Lancaster, PA independent team as well as a single A position in 2007. Tommy has also been a assistant baseball coach at a local high school for twelve seasons.

Jim Hickman

Before 1956 Season: Signed by the St. Louis Cardinals as an amateur free agent

- March 23, 1974: Traded by the Chicago Cubs to the St. Louis Cardinals for Scipio Spinks.
- July 16, 1974: Released by the St. Louis Cardinals.

It took Jim 18 seasons in professional ball before appearing with the big league team that originally signed him. "As a kid, I didn't know there was any other club than the Cardinals", noted Hickman. A member of the original New York Mets, Hickman was a full-time starter his first four years with the team. He was the first Met to hit for the cycle and the last player to homer in the Polo Grounds. His career highlight had to be the 1970 season with the Cubs. Batting a career-high .315 with 32 home runs and 115 RBI's, Hickman made his only appearance in the All Star game that season.

Hickman had the occasional start at first base, along with pinch-hitting with the Cardinals in his last season, 1974. He batted only .200 as a pinch-hitter with two home runs, .267 overall. With the club calling up youngsters from Tulsa, Jim's career ended with the team it started with. He left baseball with a career .252 average, 159 homers and 1002 hits. He did some coaching in the low minor leagues but primarily took care of his 650 acres in his hometown in Tennessee.

Dennis Higgins

- July 20, 1971: Traded by the Oakland Athletics to the St. Louis Cardinals for Gaylen Pitts.
- September 1, 1972: Purchased by the San Diego Padres from the St. Louis Cardinals.

Higgins, who compiled 29 saves for Washington in 1968/1969 (when saves were not as common) was a righthanded relief specialist who appeared in 18 games over the Redbirds 1971/72 seasons. Making his major league debut on opening day 1966, Higgins pitched 2 2/3 scoreless innings with 5 strikeouts for the White Sox. A Jefferson City, Missouri native, Higgins was sold to San Diego as part of the Cardinals youth movement, also parting with Matty Alou and Dal Maxvill during that time. He never played again.

Higgins enjoyed his time with the Redbirds, especially meeting his idol, Stan Musial. "He came into the clubhouse all the time. He'd come up to you and talk. He'd shake your hand and wouldn't let loose until he was through talking. He was really funny". Dennis was inducted into the Missouri Sports Hall of Fame in 2013.

Tom Hilgendorf

- Before 1960 Season: Signed by the St. Louis Cardinals as an amateur free agent.
- December 2, 1970: Traded by the St. Louis Cardinals to the Kansas City Royals for Ike Brookens.

Hilgendorf, a lefthanded 1960 Cardinal draftee, appeared in his first major league game in 1969. After the 1970 season, a 0-4 record and 3 saves, Hilgendorf next showed up in Cleveland where he gained notoriety by getting hit by a thrown chair during the infamous 10 cent beer night promo in 1974. After an excellent 1975 season with Philadelphia (7-3, 2.14 ERA) Tom was released before the 1976 season began. Picked up by the Pirates Charleston farm club, Tom was hit hard in a 8-run ninth inning, giving up 3 homers, 2 doubles, and a single. Asked if he had ever been rocked like that before, Tom replied "Not since my mother rocked me as a baby". His career ended with a 19-14 record and 3.04 ERA with 14 saves. Upon retirement, Tom now resides in his native Iowa.

Marc Hill

- June 4, 1970: Drafted by the St. Louis Cardinals in the 10th round of the 1970 amateur draft.
- October 14, 1974: Traded by the St. Louis Cardinals to the San Francisco Giants for Ken Rudolph and Elias Sosa.
- June 20, 1980: Purchased by the Seattle Mariners from the San Francisco Giants.

An Elsberry, Missouri native, Hill was a strong-armed, good defensive catcher with a lively clubhouse presence. A Cardinal draft choice with large prospects, Marc had only 24 at bats during the 1973/74 seasons before departing for San Francisco. A career .223 hitter over 14 seasons, Hill and Carlton Fisk combined for 27 home runs for a White Sox record for catchers in 1983. Fisk had 26 of them.

After his career ended, Marc managed in the minors for the Sox, Seattle, and Pittsburgh. He has also been a coach for the Astros in 1988 and the Yankees bullpen coach in 1991.

Doug Howard

- October 7, 1974: the California Angels sent Doug Howard to the St. Louis Cardinals to complete an earlier deal made on July 31, 1974. July 31, 1974: The California Angels sent a player to be named later to the St. Louis Cardinals for Bob Heise.
- September 30, 1975: the St. Louis Cardinals sent Doug Howard to the Cleveland Indians to complete an earlier deal made on May 27, 1975. May 27, 1975: The St. Louis Cardinals sent a player to be named later to the Cleveland Indians for Luis Alvarado.

Voted one of the top ten athletes of all time at BYU, Howard was a two-sport athlete, drafted by the Angels as well as the Chicago Bulls of the NBA. Howard played parts of five seasons in the bigs. With the Cardinals in 1975 he batted .207 in 29 at bats with his only major league home run that season. His career ended the following season in Cleveland. He left with a career .212 average and 46 big league hits. Doug was elected to the BYU Hall of Fame for his basketball prowess in 1982.

Al Hrabosky

- February 1, 1969: Drafted by the St. Louis Cardinals in the 1st round (19th pick) of the 1969 amateur draft (January).
- December 8, 1977: Traded by the St. Louis Cardinals to the Kansas City Royals for Mark Littell and Buck Martinez.

The "Mad Hungarian" began his colorful 8-year tenure with the Cardinals in 1970, gradually improving each season to a league-high 22 saves in 1975. Al became a fan favorite for his antics on the mound. Between each pitch, he would turn and walk towards second base, rub the ball several times, take a deep breath, and pound the ball into his mitt. He would then storm back to the mound, staring down the batter. After butting heads with new manager Vern Rapp's hair policy in 1977, Al was traded to Kansas City for Mark Littell after the season. After an off-season in 1979, Hrabosky cashed in on free agency, signing a multi-year deal with the Braves. Injuries and diminished opportunities curtailed his time with the Braves, retiring after the 1982 season. Al left with solid numbers over his 13 year career, 64-35 record, 3.10 ERA and 97 career saves.

A color commentator for the Cardinals television broadcasts since 1985 and a motivational speaker, Al continues to be a large cog in Cardinal nation.

Charlie Hudson

- October 18, 1971: Traded by the New York Mets with Jim Bibby, Rich Folkers and Art Shamsky to the St. Louis Cardinals for Jim Beauchamp, Chip Coulter, Harry Parker and Chuck Taylor.

- February 1, 1973: Traded by the St. Louis Cardinals with a player to be named later to the Texas Rangers for a player to be named later. The Texas Rangers sent Mike Thompson (March 31, 1973) to the St. Louis Cardinals to complete the trade. The St. Louis Cardinals sent Mike Nagy (March 31, 1973) to the Texas Rangers to complete the trade.

Not to be confused with Charles Hudson, Philly & Yankee hurler of the 80's, this Charlie Hudson appeared in only three major league seasons, including the Cardinals in 1972. A favorite of Whitey Herzog during his Mets years, Charlie was acquired by Texas after Herzog became manager. A lefthander, Charlie appeared in 12 games with the Cardinals in 1972 with a 1-0 record.

Making the 1973 Texas roster and learning the knuckleball, Hudson accidentally shot himself in his hand while cleaning a gun. He finished out the season with the Rangers, but only appeared in three more major league games after 1973, with California in 1975. Charlie pitched one additional season in the minors; his major league tenure ended with a 5-3 record and 5.04 ERA covering 40 games and 80 innings.

Terry Hughes

- April 4, 1973: Purchased by the St. Louis Cardinals from the Chicago Cubs.

- December 7, 1973: Traded by the St. Louis Cardinals with Reggie Cleveland and Diego Segui to the Boston Red Sox for John Curtis, Mike Garman and Lynn McGlothen.

- January 9, 1976: Purchased by the St. Louis Cardinals from the Boston Red Sox.

The overall 2nd pick in the 1967 draft (after Ron Bloomberg), Terry had only 86 career at bats during his major league career. During the 1973 season, Terry had a good season in AAA Tulsa, batting .289 with 10 home runs an 51 RBI's, but could not convey that to the bigs, going 3-14 with 1 RBI that year.

Hughes was traded to Boston after the season, unusual since one of the players traded to the Cardinals, Mike Garman, was drafted immediately after Hughes. He ended his pro career back in Tulsa in 1976, finishing his major league career at .209 with 18 hits. Terry lives back in his home of South Carolina.

Ron Hunt

- September 5, 1974: Selected off waivers by the St. Louis Cardinals from the Montreal Expos.
- March 26, 1975: Released by the St. Louis Cardinals.

Like Jerry Reuss, a Ritenour High School graduate, Hunt gained notoriety by his propensity of getting hit by a pitched ball. Over the course of his 12-year major league run, Hunt was hit by a pitch 243 times,(6th all-time) leading the National League seven years straight . His season-high mark was 50, set during the 1971 season. A career .273 hitter and two time All Star with the Mets in 1964 & 1966, Ron ended his career with the Cardinals in September 1974, hitting .174 in 23 at bats.

Hunt retired to the Wentzville, Missouri area where he owned a liquor store and sporting goods store before opening Ron Hunt's Instructional Baseball Camp in 1986. Ron was involved with the camp until retiring in 2003. He now enjoys his cattle, along with hunting and fishing.

Dane Iorg

- June 15, 1977: Traded by the Philadelphia Phillies with Rick Bosetti and Tom Underwood to the St. Louis Cardinals for Bake McBride and Steve Waterbury.
- May 10, 1984: Purchased by the Kansas City Royals from the St. Louis Cardinals.

A valuable utility man for the Redbirds, Iorg spent eight of his ten major league seasons with the team, batting .294 for the club overall. In the strike shortened season of 1981, Dane lead the club in batting at .327 as well as RBI's with 61. As designated hitter with the club in the 1982 World Series, Dane batted .529, earning a World Series title. He would came back to haunt the Cardinals however in 1985, while with the Royals, Dane had the game-winning hit in Game 6 of the I-70 series, earning another championship. He left the game after the 1986 season with a career .276 average.

A proud father of eight children, and member of the BYU Hall of Fame (1982), Dane lives in Salt Lake City where he works in lumber sales as well as a health and nutrition business.

Michael "Mike" Jackson

- September 13, 1971: Purchased by the St. Louis Cardinals from the Kansas City Royals.
- October 18, 1971: Returned to the Kansas City Royals by the St. Louis Cardinals following previous purchase.

No, not THAT Michael Jackson! This gloved one appeared in one game with the Redbirds in 1971 totaling 2/3 of an inning, allowing one hit and one walk. His major league career ended in Cleveland in 1973 with a career 2-3 record 5.80 ERA covering 49 2/3 innings. Mike accumulated 70 wins during his 9 season minor league career. No, I do not know if his spouse is named Billie Jean!

Julian Javier

- May 28, 1960: Traded by the Pittsburgh Pirates with Ed Bauta to the St. Louis Cardinals for Dick Gray and Vinegar Bend Mizell.
- March 24, 1972: Traded by the St. Louis Cardinals to the Cincinnati Reds for Tony Cloninger.

Julian, a 10-year starter at second base for the Redbirds in the sixties, still holds the all time record for games played at the position. A .257 career hitter with over 1400 career hits, and 1963 & 1968 All Star, Julian led the team in stolen bases from 1960-63 until some guy named Lou Brock came along. A World Series Champ in 1964 & 67, Javier retired to his Dominican Republic home, where a stadium is named in his honor. His son Stan (named after Julian's teammate Stan Musial) was a 17-year major league veteran and another son, Julian Javier Jr is a cardiac & vascular specialist who has named a non-profit foundation in his father's name.

Jerry Johnson

- October 7, 1969: Traded by the Philadelphia Phillies with Dick Allen and Cookie Rojas to the St. Louis Cardinals for Byron Browne, Curt Flood, Joe Hoerner and Tim McCarver. Curt Flood refused to report to his new team. The St. Louis Cardinals sent Willie Montanez (April 8, 1970) and Jim Browning (minors) (August 30, 1970) to the Philadelphia Phillies to complete the trade.
- May 19, 1970: Traded by the St. Louis Cardinals to the San Francisco Giants for Frank Linzy.

Johnson appeared in only 7 games with the Cardinals in 1970. He admitted he was "shocked" to be dealt to San Francisco, having pitched well for the club (2-0 3.27 ERA). Cardinal management felt Frank Linzy would be a better fit for a short reliever. Johnson subsequently had a great season with the Giants in 1971, with 18 saves as well as receiving Cy Young Award and MVP votes. Jerry ended his 11-year career with the Toronto Blue Jays in 1977, winning the first game in Blue Jay history. His career ended after that season with a 48-51 career mark and 41 saves.

Alfred "Skip" Jutze

- January 27, 1968: Drafted by the St Louis Cardinals in the 4th round of the 1968 amateur draft (January Secondary).
- November 28, 1972: Traded by the St. Louis Cardinals with Milt Ramirez to the Houston Astros for Ray Busse and Bobby Fenwick.

Skip, a highly regarded minor leaguer appeared for the Cardinals in September 1972, hitting .239 with 5 RBI's. With the prospect of playing behind Ted Simmons, Skip was traded to Houston, where he served for four part-time seasons. Skip ended his career with the expansion Seattle Mariners in 1977, hitting the team's first grand slam home run. He finished with a career .215 average and 141 hits.

With a degree in Industrial Education, Skip retired from baseball to work for Jeffco, a Colorado company that provides vocational training and job placement for the developmentally disabled.

Michael (Mick) Kelleher

- June 5, 1969: Drafted by the St. Louis Cardinals in the 3rd round of the 1969 amateur draft. Player signed June 17, 1969.
- October 23, 1973: Purchased by the Houston Astros from the St. Louis Cardinals.
- December 13, 1974: Purchased by the St. Louis Cardinals from the Houston Astros.
- December 22, 1975: Traded by the St. Louis Cardinals to the Chicago Cubs for Vic Harris.

Mick, a career .213 hitter in an 11-year major league career, was a good fielding infielder with no power. Since his retirement as a player in 1982, no major league player (non-pitcher) has accrued as many at bats without a home run. He batted .162 in parts of three seasons with the Redbirds.

Upon his retirement, Mick served in many coaching capacities, primarily as a fielding instructor for numerous organizations. As of 2012, Mick has served as the Yankees first base coach and fielding instructor for the last four years, earning a World Series ring in 2009.

James Kennedy

- December 1, 1969: Drafted by the St. Louis Cardinals from the New York Yankees in the 1969 rule 5 draft.
- October 20, 1970: Traded by the St. Louis Cardinals with Sal Campisi to the Minnesota Twins for Charlie Wissler (minors) and Herman Hill.

Called up twice to the Redbirds during 1970, Kennedy batted .125 in 25 at bats, no RBI's and 2 errors. His major league career ended after 12 games at shortstop and second. James bounced around the high minor leagues before concluding his eight season professional career after the 1973 season. James is the brother of former Cincinnati and Cub infielder Junior, who played from 1974-83.

Terry Kennedy

- June 7, 1977: Drafted by the St. Louis Cardinals in the 1st round (6th pick) of the 1977 amateur draft.
- December 8, 1980: Traded by the St. Louis Cardinals with John Littlefield, Al Olmsted, Mike Phillips, Kim Seaman, Steve Swisher and John Urrea to the San Diego Padres for a player to be named later, Rollie Fingers, Bob Shirley and Gene Tenace. The San Diego Padres sent Bob Geren (December 10, 1980) to the St. Louis Cardinals to complete the trade.

Playing behind stalwart Ted Simmons, Kennedy had few opportunities to catch during his stay from 1978-1980. He hit .284 in 109 at bats in 1979 and .254 with 4 dingers and 34 RBI's the following season. He got his break that offseason, Simmons was traded to Milwaukee, four days after Kennedy was traded to San Diego. Kennedy made the most of his starting role with the Padres, hitting .301 in his first year, 1981 and being named MVP of the club in 1982 with a .295 average, 21 homers and 97 ribbies. An All Star with the Padres for three seasons, along with a 1983 Silver Slugger Award, Terry became the first father/son combination to get a RBI in World Series play that year. His father, Bob, played in the American League in the 1950's. He earned another All Star appearance with Baltimore in 1987 before winding up his 14-year career in 1991 with a .264 cumulative average.

Terry has either managed, coached or instructed at the minor league level for nearly twenty years with numerous organizations, including the Cardinals. Terry and his wife are both real estate agents in the Tucson area as well. He was named "Baseball America" Manager of the Year in 1998 for his efforts with the Iowa Cubs. Terry recently managed Tucson in the Padres organization during the 2012 season.

Don Kessinger

- October 28, 1975: Traded by the Chicago Cubs to the St. Louis Cardinals for a player to be named later and Mike Garman. The St. Louis Cardinals sent Bobby Hrapmann (minors) (April 5, 1976) to the Chicago Cubs to complete the trade.
- August 20, 1977: Traded by the St. Louis Cardinals to the Chicago White Sox for Steve Staniland (minors).

The long-time Chicago Cub was brought into the fold in 1976 after the failed Ed Brinkman experiment of the previous season. While hitting only .239 for the Cardinals in both 1976 & '77, Don provided stability at shortstop and was a valuable teacher for Garry Templeton, who would take over the position. Don also helped out at third and

DON KESSINGER   INFIELDER

second base before going to the other Chicago organization in August of 1977.

A six-time All Star and two time Gold Glove, Don ended his 16-year career (.239) as player-coach with the White Sox in 1979.

Managing was not to his liking. Don resigned before the season ended, being replaced by some guy named Tony LaRussa.

Don replaced former major leaguer Jake Gibbs as baseball coach at the University of Mississippi, where he coached six seasons. He spent another four years in the athletic department. A member of the Cubs, Ole Miss and Arkansas Hall of Fame, Don is President of Kessinger Real Estate in Oxford, Mississippi.

Darold Knowles

- January 16, 1979: Signed as a Free Agent with the St. Louis Cardinals.
- May 9, 1980: Released by the St. Louis Cardinals.

One of the few free agent signings by the club in that era, Knowles was near the end of a distinguished 16-year career. Primarily a lefty reliever, Knowles made his only All Star appearance in 1969 finishing that season with a 9-2 record, 2.24 ERA and 13 saves. That was followed by a horrific 2-14 1970 won/loss record, but with a 2.04 ERA and 27 saves. Knowles was a key lefthander out of the bullpen during the Swingin A's 1972-74 era, appearing in all seven games of the 1973 World Series. Because of injuries to the staff in '73, Knowles started five games, pitching a 6-hit shutout in one.

Knowles did not distinguish himself with the Cardinals, going 2-5 in 1979 with a 4.07 ERA and 6 saves, including two trick pickoff plays that turned ugly and only two games the following year before his career ended with a 66-74 record, a fine 3.12 ERA and 143 saves. After staying in the Redbird organization, Darold was the pitching coach for the 1983 team before moving on to the Phillies organization as pitching coach from 1988-1990. After later stops in the Phillies and Pirates minor leagues, Knowles landed in Dunedin, where he has resided since 2006 as the Blue Jays pitching coach.

Lew Krausse

- September 1, 1973: Purchased with Larry Haney by the St. Louis Cardinals from the Oakland Athletics.
- October 26, 1973: Released by the St. Louis Cardinals.

The first of A's owner Charlie Finley's bonus babies, Krausse signed a $125,000 bonus right after high school in 1961 and shut out the Angels on 6 hits a week later. Son of Lew Krausse, also a pitcher for the A's (1931-32) he started the first game in Milwaukee Brewer history. A 12-year major league veteran, Krausse had a poor 68-91 won-loss ledger, but pitched on some poor teams in the late sixties, early seventies. He enjoyed three 10+ victory seasons and 21 career saves. Near the end of his career in 1973, Lew appeared in only one game with the Cardinals covering only 2 innings.

After his playing days, Lew remained in the Kansas City area, operating a metal business in the area, which is still run by his family today. In retirement, Lew has appeared at reunions with the A's and Brewers organizations.

Ted Kubiak

- July 29, 1971: Traded by the Milwaukee Brewers with Charlie Loseth (minors) to the St. Louis Cardinals for Jose Cardenal, Bob Reynolds and Dick Schofield.
- November 3, 1971: Traded by the St. Louis Cardinals to the Texas Rangers for Joe Grzenda.

Kubiak, a versatile, average fielding infielder made his mark during his short time with the club in 1971. Kubiak batted .250 and blasted a three-run homer to seal Bob Gibson's 200 career victory. Ted still shares the Milwaukee Brewers record with 7 RBI's in one game and won three World Series rings with the A's from 1972-74. His ten-year career lasted until 1976 with a career mark of .231, enjoying only one season as a regular in 1970 with the Brewers, hitting .252 with 41 RBI's.

Upon the conclusion of his career, Ted did color commentary for the A's television network in 1978 before becoming involved in real estate and renovation of houses and apartments. In 1989, baseball came calling again. Since that year, Kubiak has managed for the A's organization (1989-1993), as well as the Indians to the present day.

Ryan Kurosaki

- Before 1974 Season: Signed by the St. Louis Cardinals as an amateur free agent.

The first Asian-American to play in the majors, Kurosaki pitched in 7 games with the Cards in 1975. The Hawaii native, a high school teammate of future Oriole Lenn Sakata allowed 3 home runs in 13 innings for a career ERA of 7.62. His professional career ended in 1980 with the Cardinals Springfield affiliate after a promising 7-year minor league tenure, recording a 41-29 record, 3.21 ERA and 53 saves, all of them in the Redbirds organization.

Ryan moved to Arkansas after his career ended, where he became a fireman for the city of Little Rock.

Lerrin LaGrow

- April 2, 1976: Purchased by the St. Louis Cardinals from the Detroit Tigers.
- March 23, 1977: Traded by the St. Louis Cardinals to the Chicago White Sox for Clay Carroll.

LaGrow will be most remembered for his pitch that hit the A's Burt Campaneris in the ankle during the 1972 A.L.Championship Series. "Campy" promptly picked up his bat and hurled it at LaGrow, missing him by inches. Both were suspended for the remainder of the series. Lerrin came to the Redbirds after two poor seasons for bad Tiger clubs, an 8-19 record in 1974 and 7-14 in 1975. His time with the Cards was brief- 8 games, 2 starts, 1 complete game and a 0-1 record and 1.48 ERA. He was traded after competing for a spot on the 1977 roster.

His best season was with the Sox, saving 25 games in '77 with a 7-3 record, along with 16 saves the following year. He was released by Philadelphia mid-season 1980, ending his 10 seasons in the majors with a 34-55 mark, 4.11 ERA and 54 saves.

Investing in real estate during his playing days, Lerrin has been involved as a business broker since 1981. He is a member of the Executive Association of Greater Phoenix.

Leron Lee

- June 7, 1966: Drafted by the St. Louis Cardinals in the 1st round (7th pick) of the 1966 amateur draft.
- June 11, 1971: Traded by the St. Louis Cardinals with Fred Norman to the San Diego Padres for Al Santorini.

A 1966 first round draft pick by the Cardinals, Lee batted .222 for the team between 1969-1971, primarily as a utility and spot starter in the outfield. His best major league season was in 1972 with San Diego, where he batted .300, the only season where he exceeded 400 at bats. After the '76 season with Los Angeles and the Mexican League, Lee's career took him East-the Far East. Leron was the first American ballplayer (or "gaijin') to play and live in Japan during his prime as a player, and the results were impressive.

A ten-year career ensued in Japan, with upwards of four times the income Lee was earning stateside. A near triple crown his first season, a .320 career average that tops the league all time (for a minimum of 400 at bats), still in the top ten all time for homers, total bases and RBI's. After returning to the U.S., Lee helped the 1989 A's earn a World Series ring as batting coach and later has scouted in the Cincinnati and Atlanta organizations.

Jim Lentine

- June 3, 1975: Drafted by the St. Louis Cardinals in the 12th round of the 1975 amateur draft.
- June 2, 1980: Traded by the St. Louis Cardinals to the Detroit Tigers for Al Greene and John Martin.

Called up late in the 1978 season based on his .342 average in AA Springfield, Lentine was hit by pitch in his first major league at bat. An eight-year veteran of the minors, Jim was recalled again late in 1979 and went 9 for 23, hitting .391. That late season performance earned Lentine a spot on the 1980 opening day roster. He got only 10 at bats, with a hit before being traded for lefty John Martin. He ended his major league career that season with a total of 205 at bats and a .263 average.

Lertine became a scout for the Texas Rangers after baseball as well as a hitting instructor. He is now a principal of West Coast Sports Management based in Pasadena, California.

Barry Lersch

- September 14, 1974: Purchased by the St. Louis Cardinals from the Atlanta Braves.

Acquired late in the 1974 season, Lersch was in one game with the Cardinals, pitching 1 1/3 innings, giving up 3 hits and 6 runs for a ERA of 40.50. That was the last major league appearance for Larry. The starting pitcher for the Phillies last game at Connie Mack Stadium, Barry had a 18-32 career record and 3.82 ERA in the majors between 1969 and 1974, including a 5-14 record as a starter with the Phillies in 1971. He died of a heart attack in 2009 at the age of 65.

Larry Lintz

- July 25, 1975: Traded by the Montreal Expos to the St. Louis Cardinals for Jim Dwyer.
- October 28, 1975: Traded by the St. Louis Cardinals to the Oakland Athletics for Charlie Chant.

Lintz was a speedster throughout his 6-year career, once stealing 96 bases in 1972 before earning his promotion to the Expos the following season. Though his career average was a middling .227, Larry managed to reach base often and swiped 50 bases with the Expos in 1974.

His time with the Cardinals was brief, 27 games in 1975, a .278 average and four stolen bases. Lintz sealed his fate with the club when he refused to attend the Florida Instructional League to work on his hitting and bunting. In Oakland, Lintz stole 32 bases as a designated runner in 1976, appearing at the plate only once all season. After a more traditional role the next year and a .133 average and 13 stolen bases, Lintz played only three more games in the majors after that.

Frank Linzy

- May 19, 1970: Traded by the San Francisco Giants to the St. Louis Cardinals for Jerry Johnson.
- March 26, 1972: Traded by the St. Louis Cardinals to the Milwaukee Brewers for Rich Stonum (minors).

Frank Linzy's acquisition and departure seemed curious to me. Jerry Johnson had a very good 1970 season for the Redbirds but was traded for Linzy, who was carrying an ERA over 7 with the Giants. Frank had an excellent season in 1971 with a 4-3 record, 2.12 ERA and 6 saves in 50 games. However, in late spring 1972, he was practically given away during a Cardinals housecleaning of their bullpen.

A good sinkerball pitcher, Linzy had a great rookie year with the Giants in 1965, recording 21 saves. He ended his 11-year career with a 62-57 record, 111 saves and a 2.85 ERA. Now retired in his native Oklahoma, Frank enjoys nothing more than fishing these days.

Mark Littell

- December 8, 1977: Traded by the Kansas City Royals with Buck Martinez to the St. Louis Cardinals for Al Hrabosky.

"Country" is famously known by Yankees fans as the reliever who gave up the game winning, series clinching dinger against Chris Chambliss in the 1976 A.L. Championship series. He had two very good seasons in Kansas City in 1976 & '77, earning an 8-4 record with

16 and 12 saves, respectively. Acquired for fan favorite Al Hrabosky, Mark improved on a choppy 1978 season with a solid, 9-4, 2.19 ERA and 13 saves in 1979. Bone spurs and eventual surgery took their toll, he accumulated only 4 more saves before being out of baseball at the end of the 1982 season. Mark ended with a career 32-31 mark and 56 saves.

Mark coached for 18 seasons after his career stalled, with San Diego, Milwaukee, LA, and Kansas City. In 2006, Mark introduced the "Nutty Buddy" (look for it on YouTube), a protective athletic cup. Mark takes a fastball from a pitching machine right on his "boys" to show the effectiveness of the device. Mark, "The best compliment I ever got was from the mother of an 11-year-old boy who said that he fell asleep in his Nutty Buddy. In 2012, Mark Littell was appointed assistant coach for the Dickinson State baseball team in North Dakota. Insert joke here......

Aurelio Lopez

- October 26, 1977: Purchased by the St. Louis Cardinals from Mexico City Reds (Mexican).
- December 4, 1978: Traded by the St. Louis Cardinals with Jerry Morales to the Detroit Tigers for Jack Murphy (minors) and Bob Sykes.

"Senior Smoke," a pudgy competitor appeared in 25 games with the Redbirds in 1978, compiling a 4-2 record. His greatest success came in his 7 seasons with the Tigers, including an 18- save season and All Star selection in 1983 followed by a brilliant 10-1 1984 year with a 2.94 ERA, 14 saves and a World Series ring. He completed his 11th season major league career in 1987 with Houston, ending with a 62-36 record and 85 saves.

Retiring to his hometown of Tecamachalco, Mexico, Aurelio became municipal president (similar to mayor) of the area in 1990. An auto accident two years later claimed his life at the age of 44. Lopez was posthumously elected into the Mexican Hall of Fame in 1993.

Orlando "Marty" Martinez

- November 3, 1971: Traded by the Houston Astros to the St. Louis Cardinals for Bob Stinson.
- May 18, 1972: Traded by the St. Louis Cardinals to the Oakland Athletics for Brant Alyea. Brant Alyea returned to original team on July 23, 1972.

In the final season of his 7-year career, Marty had 3 hits in 7 at bats with the club in 1972 along with 2 RBI's after going only 1 for 25 in spring training that season.

A career .243 who could play practically every position, Marty joined Mick Kelleher as players who had no "dingers" during their major league career. He followed up his career by coaching in the Texas and Seattle organizations, managing the Mariners in 1986 for 1 game as interim manager. Marty passed away from a heart attack in the Dominican Republic in 2007 at the age of 65.

Silvio Martinez

- November 28, 1977: the Chicago White Sox sent Dave Hamilton and Silvio Martinez to the St. Louis Cardinals to complete an earlier deal made on August 31, 1977.
- August 31, 1977: The Chicago White Sox sent players to be named later to the St. Louis Cardinals for Clay Carroll.
- November 20, 1981: Traded as part of a 3-team trade by the St. Louis Cardinals with Lary Sorensen to the Cleveland Indians. The Cleveland Indians sent Bo Diaz to the Philadelphia Phillies. The Philadelphia Phillies sent a player to be named later to the Cleveland Indians. The Philadelphia Phillies sent Lonnie Smith to the St. Louis Cardinals. The Philadelphia Phillies sent Scott Munninghoff (December 9, 1981) to the Cleveland Indians to complete the trade.

In his final minor league start with the Cardinals AAA Springfield affiliate, Silvio threw a no hitter. In his first big league start after being called up, Silvio hurled a complete game one-hitter against the Mets. Six weeks later, Silvio tossed another complete game one hitter. That does not include the two two-hitters he had in his debut season, ending with a 9-8 record, 3.64 ERA and 2 shutouts. 1979 was better yet , tied with Bob Forsch with 15 victories, a 3.27 ERA and another two shutouts.

The bright light started to fade at that point. Missing two weeks of spring training due to pneumonia, Silvio injured his arm and back, dropping to 5-10 with nearly a 5.00 ERA. After only two wins in 1981, Silvio was traded, never to see the majors again, ending his five-year career with a 31-32 record and 3.88 ERA.

Ted Martinez

- December 11, 1974: Traded by the New York Mets to the St. Louis Cardinals for Jack Heidemann and Mike Vail.
- May 18, 1975: Traded by the St. Louis Cardinals to the Oakland Athletics for a player to be named later and Steve Staniland (minors). The Oakland Athletics sent Mike Barlow (May 23, 1975) to the St. Louis Cardinals to complete the trade.

Picked up from the Mets because of his versatility, Martinez batted only .190 during his two-month stay with the team. After his indecision in scoring from third base and being tagged out, Teddy was traded the following day to Oakland. A valuable infield backup for the Mets, Martinez lead the team in triples in 1972 & '74. His three years with the Dodgers at the end of his career were his best, batting .280 for his time there, a 40 point increase of his career .240 average. Martinez later coached and managed in the Dodger organization including coaching a team in the Chinese (Taiwan) Professional Baseball League.

Dal Maxvill

- Before 1960 Season: Signed by the St. Louis Cardinals as an amateur free agent.
- August 30, 1972: Traded by the St. Louis Cardinals to the Oakland Athletics for a player to be named later and Joe Lindsey (minors). The Oakland Athletics sent Gene Dusen (minors) (October 27, 1972) to the St. Louis Cardinals to complete the trade.

Maxvill, a Granite City native and Wash U grad (engineering), was a fixture at shortstop during his 11-year tenure with the club. A decent fielding light hitter, Dal earned four World Series titles during his career, 2 with the Cards (1964 & 67) and 2 with the A's (1972 & 74). A career .217 hitter in 14 major league seasons, Dal hit the first major league grand slam on Canadian soil in 1969.

Maxvill later served as a coach with the Cardinals, Mets and Braves (where he served along with Bob Gibson, on Joe Torres' staff). In 1985, he became general manager of the Cardinals for the next decade, and the team won two more pennants in 1985 and 1987. After his resignation in 1994, Maxvill scouted for the Yankees.

Will McEnaney

- February 19, 1979: Signed as a Free Agent with the St. Louis Cardinals.
- March 31, 1980: Released by the St. Louis Cardinals.

Part of the Reds "Big Red Machine" in 1975, the lefty reliever McEnaney saved Game 7 of the historic 1975 World Series as well as two Series games the following year against the Yankees. Will made 52 consecutive appearances in 1975 before giving up a home run. A free spirit in the minor leagues in Indianapolis, Will liked to walk his imaginary dog outside the clubhouse. Future Cardinal Manager Vern

Rapp, growing frustrated, snapped, "McEnaney, get that damned dog inside!"

Called up in May 1979 to the Cardinals, Will recorded a 0-3 record, 2.95 ERA and 2 saves in 45 appearances. Somewhat surprisingly, Will was one of the final cuts in 1980, never appearing in the big leagues again. His career ended with a 12-17 record, 3.76 ERA and 29 saves.

Will has worn many hats after his career ended in the minors in 1985, including, car dealer, painting contractor, and investment banker. For twelve years he managed a company that refinishes bathroom tiles before returning to the game as the scoreboard operator at Roger Dean Stadium in Jupiter, Florida.

Arnold "Bake" McBride

BAKE McBRIDE   OUTFIELDER

- June 4, 1970: Drafted by the St. Louis Cardinals in the 37th round of the 1970 amateur draft.
- June 15, 1977: Traded by the St. Louis Cardinals with Steve Waterbury to the Philadelphia Phillies for Rick Bosetti, Dane Iorg and Tom Underwood.

The epitome of 70's cool, Bake McBride had the look; long and lanky with the large Afro puffing out from his cap and thick mutton chops. Smooth on the field and faster on the bases, Bake gained notoriety scoring from first base on a errant pick-off in the 25th inning game against the Mets in 1974. A .307 hitter for his 5 years with the Cardinals, Bake won the Rookie of the Year in the Cardinals near-miss in 1974.

After an All Star appearance in 1976, Bake was traded in another of the organizations ill-fated decisions. McBride contributed greatly to the Phillies first World Championship in 1980 (10th in MVP votes) before knee and leg injuries started taking their toll.

After his career concluded in 1984 with a career .299 average, Bake held the minor league base running coach position in the Mets organization.

Tim McCarver

- June 8, 1959: Signed by the St. Louis Cardinals as an amateur free agent.
- October 7, 1969: Traded by the St. Louis Cardinals with Byron Browne, Curt Flood and Joe Hoerner to the Philadelphia Phillies for Dick Allen, Jerry Johnson and Cookie Rojas. Curt Flood refused to report to his new team. The St. Louis Cardinals sent Willie Montanez (April 8, 1970) and Jim Browning (minors) (August 30, 1970) to the Philadelphia Phillies to complete the trade.
- November 6, 1972: Traded by the Montreal Expos to the St. Louis Cardinals for Jorge Roque.
- September 1, 1974: Purchased by the Boston Red Sox from the St. Louis Cardinals.

The only catcher in modern baseball history to play in four decades (50's-80's), McCarver enjoyed a 21-year career, the first 12 with the Cardinals. Tim was the starting catcher from 1963-69, earning World Series rings in 64 & 67, an All-Star appearance in sweltering Busch Stadium in 1966, and runner-up to teammate and MVP Orlando Cepeda.

Tim returned to the club in 1973 with a .266 average and 49 RBI's, his most since the 1969 season. McCarver wrapped up his long career by being the personal catcher for his old teammate Steve Carlton in Philadelphia. His baseball intellect came in handy in his new career in baseball broadcasting. A broadcaster since 1983 for the Mets, Giants,

Yankees and Phillies followed with all four major networks. In 2012, Tim was inducted in the broadcast wing of the Baseball Hall of Fame.

Bill McCool

- April 2, 1970: Traded by the <u>San Diego Padres</u> to the <u>St. Louis Cardinals</u> for <u>Steve Huntz</u>.
- October 6, 1970: Traded by the <u>St. Louis Cardinals</u> to the <u>Boston Red Sox</u> for <u>Bill Landis</u>. (Date given is approximate. Exact date is uncertain.)

Another great name in Cardinal history, McCool should have been discovered hanging out with the "Fonz" of Happy Days Fame. This hard throwing left-hander enjoyed a 21 save season at the age of 20, and made the All Star game in 1966 with the Reds based on a 2.48 ERA and another 18 save ledger. A wrist injury effected the balance of his career, including being drafted as one of the original San Diego Padres.

His time with the Redbirds was brief, a 0-3 record, 6.23 ERA in 18 games in 1970. His professional career ended the following season. Now retired in Florida, Billy was elected to the Indiana Baseball Hall of Fame in 2012.

Lynn McGlothen

- December 7, 1973: Traded by the Boston Red Sox with John Curtis and Mike Garman to the St. Louis Cardinals for Reggie Cleveland, Terry Hughes and Diego Segui.
- December 10, 1976: Traded by the St. Louis Cardinals to the San Francisco Giants for Ken Reitz.

A dependable starter for the Redbirds between 1974 & '76, McGlothen won 44 games (and lost 40) with a 3.49 ERA and 9 shutouts during his run with the team. The opening day starter in 1976, replacing the departed Bob Gibson, McGlothen pitched a complete game shutout. An All Star in his first season with the club, Lynn was dealt to the Giants to reacquire Ken Reitz. Lynn pitched six more seasons in the majors, winning 33 more games before ending his career at the conclusion of the 1982 season. His career ended with an 86-93 record and five seasons with 12 or more victories. Sadly, Lynn perished, along with a woman who was trying to save him, in a mobile home fire in 1984, two years after his retirement.

Jerry McNertney

- October 20, 1970: Traded by the Milwaukee Brewers with Jesse Huggins (minors) and George Lauzerique to the St. Louis Cardinals for Jim Ellis and Carl Taylor.
- October 27, 1972: Released by the St. Louis Cardinals.

Jerry batted a solid .289 in 1971 with the club, known as the "Weekend Warrior" while subbing for starter Ted Simmons, who had Army reserve obligations. A clutch hitter that season, Jerry was released by the organization after a dropoff in production in 1972. His nine year career ended the following year with a .237 career average over nine seasons.

A member of the original Seattle Pilots, Jerry coached in the minor leagues before becoming bullpen coach with both the Yankees and

Red Sox. At the conclusion of his career, Jerry returned to his alma mater Iowa State (Hall of Fame 2006) to assist with the baseball program from 1989-1996

Sam Mejias

- June 23, 1976: the Milwaukee Brewers sent Sam Mejias to the St. Louis Cardinals to complete an earlier deal made on June 7, 1976. June 7, 1976: The Milwaukee Brewers sent a player to be named later to the St. Louis Cardinals for Danny Frisella.
- November 6, 1976: Traded by the St. Louis Cardinals with Bill Greif and Angel Torres to the Montreal Expos for Steve Dunning, Pat Scanlon and Tony Scott.

Brought up to the Cardinals after batting .323 at Tulsa, utility outfielder Sam made his major league debut in September 1976 batting .143 in 21 at bats with 2 stolen bases. A solid defensive outfielder with speed, Mejias never had more than 108 at bats in a season in his six years in the bigs. He concluded his career with Cincinnati in 1981 with a career 247 average.

Sam managed in the Reds minor league system for seven seasons after leaving the majors and was a coach for the Seattle Mariners from 1993-1999. He joined the Orioles organization in 2007 after managing a Phillies affiliate in the Dominican Summer League for a number of seasons.

Luis Melendez

- Before 1968 Season: Signed by the St. Louis Cardinals as an amateur free agent.
- May 19, 1976: Traded by the St. Louis Cardinals to the San Diego Padres for Bill Greif.

A reliable spare in the outfield and pinch hitter, Luis enjoyed a 7 year career with the team. A good runner and fielder, Melendez had his best seasons in 1973 and 1975, batting .267 and .265 respectively. His career lasted eight major league seasons, with a career .248 mark and 366 hits, all but 29 with the Redbirds. Upon the conclusion of his career, Luis became a coach and manager in the Cardinals and Phillies organizations in addition to the Puerto Rico baseball league. He was most recently a coach for the Phillies Gold Coast team from 2005-2009.

Clarence "Butch" Metzger

- May 17, 1977: Traded by the San Diego Padres to the St. Louis Cardinals for John D'Acquisto and Pat Scanlon.
- April 5, 1978: Selected off waivers by the New York Mets from the St. Louis Cardinals.

The 1976 National League co-Rookie of the Year with San Diego (along with Pat Zachry), had a career-year with a 11-4 record, 2.92 ERA and 16 saves. He tied a league record of winning his first 12 decisions of his pitching career. Control issues started to plague him the following season, (along with the acquisition of ace Rollie Fingers), resulting in the Cardinals obtaining him early in 1977. Butch had a excellent second half of the season, recording a 4-2 record, 3.11 ERA and 7 saves, (the last of his career) in 58 games. He could not replicate his success after that. He spent two seasons in the minor leagues before "hanging them up" after 1980. His five years in the bigs yielded a 18-9 record with 23 saves in 191 appearances, all but one in a relief role.

Butch now scouts for the Texas Rangers in the Northern California region. He has been involved in youth baseball and pitching instruction for over thirty years.

Tommy Moore

- October 13, 1974: Traded by the New York Mets with Ray Sadecki to the St. Louis Cardinals for Joe Torre.
- June 4, 1975: Traded by the St. Louis Cardinals with Ed Brinkman to the Texas Rangers for Willie Davis.

Originally an outfielder, Moore was converted to a pitcher with the Mets on the suggestion of former Cardinals manager Whitey Herzog. Out of options when acquired by the Cardinals, Moore made the opening day roster with the club in 1975. He did not last long; soon he was packaged in the deal for Willie Davis. He left with a 3.86 ERA in 10 games covering 18 2/3 innings. His career ended in 1977 with the expansion Seattle Mariners and a career record of 2-4 and 5.40 ERA over parts of four seasons and 42 games.

Jerry Morales

- December 8, 1977: Traded by the Chicago Cubs with Steve Swisher and cash to the St. Louis Cardinals for Hector Cruz and Dave Rader.
- December 4, 1978: Traded by the St. Louis Cardinals with Aurelio Lopez to the Detroit Tigers for Jack Murphy (minors) and Bob Sykes.

A consistent .270 hitter during his days with the Cubs, including a 91 RBI season in 1975 and All Star appearance in 1977, Jerry was a disappointment with the Cardinals in 1978. Jerry never seemed to fully bounce back after being hit in the knee in the All Star game, as well as a back injury and broken finger later in the 1977 season. Batting only .239 with 4 homers and 46 RBI's, including a 1 for 28 spell, Jerry missed the dimensions of the friendly confines of Wrigley Field. After a season with both the Tigers and Mets, Jerry returned to the Cubs for the final three seasons of his 15 year career, ending with a .259 average.

From 1984-86 Jerry was the Cubs minor league hitting and outfield instructor before becoming a scout for the Dodgers from 1987-1990. In addition to many seasons coaching in the Puerto Rican Winter League, Jerry was the first base and outfield coach for Montreal 2002-2004, as well as the first base coach for Washington in 2007-2008. He was most recently a coach in the Mets organization.

Jerry Mumphrey

- June 8, 1971: Drafted by the St. Louis Cardinals in the 4th round of the 1971 amateur draft.
- December 7, 1979: Traded by the St. Louis Cardinals with John Denny to the Cleveland Indians for Bobby Bonds.

After brief appearances with the team in 1974 & '75, Mumphrey was in the majors to stay by 1976, becoming the teams fourth outfielder. A switch hitter with good speed, Jerry stole 22 bases in each of his first seasons with the club as well as batting .287 in 1977. In what has to be ranked as another of the teams' worst deals, the Cards swapped Mumphrey AND John Denny for a washed-up Bobby Bonds.

Jerry had a 52 stolen base season in 1980 before heading to the Yankees for two consecutive .300+ seasons. An All Star in 1984 with Houston based on his .290 average and 83 RBI season before wrapping up his career as a excellent pinch-hitter with the Cubs, Mumphrey played 15 seasons in the majors, batting a solid .289 with over 1400 hits and 174 swipes.

Jerry currently lives in Texas and is involved in various enterprises.

Tom Murphy

- May 8, 1973: Traded by the Kansas City Royals to the St. Louis Cardinals for Al Santorini.
- December 8, 1973: Traded by the St. Louis Cardinals to the Milwaukee Brewers for Bob Heise.

A 16 game winner with the California Angels in 1970, Murphy was a fifth starter for the Redbirds in his only season with the club in 1973. Owner of a 3-7 mark with a 3.76 ERA, Murphy was sent to the bullpen in September, where he remained the rest of his career. Sporting back- to- back 20 save seasons with Milwaukee in 1974 & 75, Murphy remained in the game until 1979. His twelve season career ended with a 68-101 record, 3.78 ERA and 59 saves.

Living in California after his retirement from baseball, Murphy worked at a real estate brokerage firm and has been a part of Baseball Ambassadors, an organization spreading goodwill and baseball skills to the premier baseball team in Moscow, Russia.

Mike Nagy

- January 24, 1973: Traded by the Boston Red Sox to the St. Louis Cardinals for a player to be named later. The St. Louis Cardinals sent Lance Clemons (March 29, 1973) to the Boston Red Sox to complete the trade.

- March 31, 1973: the St. Louis Cardinals sent Mike Nagy to the Texas Rangers to complete an earlier deal made on February 1, 1973. February 1, 1973: The St. Louis Cardinals sent a player to be named later and Charlie Hudson to the Texas Rangers for a player to be named later.

- June 6, 1973: Traded by the Texas Rangers with John Wockenfuss to the St. Louis Cardinals for Jim Bibby.

- December 9, 1973: Traded by the St. Louis Cardinals to the Houston Astros for Jay Schlueter.

Nagy almost made the opening day roster in 1973, having been beaten out of a spot by Jim Bibby. He was quickly traded to Texas, then returned in June in a trade for, you guessed it, Jim Bibby. The 1969 A.L. Rookie of the Year runner-up, Nagy had a 12-2 record with Boston that season. He won only 8 more games over the next 5+ seasons, arm problems a large factor. After starting 7 of his 9 appearances with the Redbirds in '73 with a 0-2 record in 40 2/3 innnings, he was dispatched at the conclusion of the season. His six year tenure in the majors ended the following season with a final career mark of 20-13, 4.15 ERA. After 4 seasons in the Mexican League where he enjoyed success, Nagy earned his real estate brokerage license.

Mike, who still loves the game and loved his time with the Cardinals, now operates Michael T. Realty in Bronx, New York.

Fred Norman

- September 28, 1970: Selected off waivers by the St. Louis Cardinals from the Los Angeles Dodgers.
- June 11, 1971: Traded by the St. Louis Cardinals with Leron Lee to the San Diego Padres for Al Santorini.

Norman, a 5'8" lefthander, appeared in only 5 games covering 4 2/3 innings and a 9.64 ERA with the Redbirds in 1970/71. During his minor league career with the Cardinals AAA Tulsa club, Norman resurrected his screwball with the help of manager (and Hall of Famer) Warren Spahn. Shortly before his trade to San Diego that season, Norman twirled a no-hitter, coming within one walk of a perfect game.

His career took off after his acquisition by the Reds, where he enjoyed 7 consecutive 11-wins or better seasons, as well as earning World Series rings in 1975 & 76. Fred won 85 of his career 104 victories with the Reds. He retired after one season in Montreal in 1980.

Joe Nossek

- July 12, 1969: Traded by the Oakland Athletics to the St. Louis Cardinals for Bob Johnson.
- February 4, 1971: Purchased by the Milwaukee Brewers from the St. Louis Cardinals.

A career .228 hitter over a 6-year career, Joe appeared in only 10 games with the club, 9 of them in 1969. Joe was one for six in his brief stint with the Cardinals. One of his claims to fame is his 2 hits off Sandy Koufax in the 1965 World Series. The other is his affinity for stealing signs as a coach after his playing days ended. Nossek spent thirty-two seasons in baseball as a player, minor league manager and coach. Joe worked in the Milwaukee, Minnesota and Kansas City organizations before winding up his career with the White Sox, primarily as bench coach. He was most recently a scout for the Houston organization.

Rich Nye

- December 4, 1969: Traded by the Chicago Cubs to the St. Louis Cardinals for Boots Day.
- May 15, 1970: Purchased by the Montreal Expos from the St. Louis Cardinals.

Nye's 5- year major league career was nearing the end when he pitched 8 innings over 6 games with a 4.50 ERA with the Redbirds in 1970. A 13 game winner with the Cubs in 1967, the 6'4" left-hander would end his professional career in the minor leagues the following season with a rotator cuff injury. He concluded his career with a 26-31 record and 3.71 ERA. In 1972 Rich was accepted into the University of Illinois School of Veterinary Medicine, graduating in 1976.

Nye was a practicing partner in the Midwest Bird & Exotic Animal Hospital for 19 years and continues to practice and teach student interns at the Ness Exotic Wellness Center in the greater Chicago area.

Ken Oberkfell

- May 4, 1975: Signed by the St. Louis Cardinals as an amateur free agent.
- June 15, 1984: Traded by the St. Louis Cardinals to the Atlanta Braves for Ken Dayley and Mike Jorgensen.

The Highland, Illinois native played the first eight years of his 16 year career with the Redbirds from 1977-1984. A consistent .290-.300 hitter, Ken had a solid glove, leading second basemen in fielding in 1979. With his switch to third base after the trade of Ken Reitz, Ken lead third basemen in fielding in both 1982 & '83. He left the Redbirds in mid-1984, with a solid .292 average and a World Series title. "Obie" enjoyed some fine seasons in Atlanta as well before playing the last five seasons in a utility role, ending with a career .278 average and over 1300 hits.

Oberkfell remains in the game today, managing for over 15 years in the minor leagues. After a stint in the Phillies organization from 1997-2000, Ken managed in the Mets AAA affiliate for six seasons, earning Baseball Americas Minor League Manager of the Year in 2005. A bench coach for the Mets in 2011, Ken has been considered for the Mets managing job over the years, but was always rebuffed. He managed the Newark minor league team in 2012 (replaced in 2013 by Garry Templeton) and currently manages the Lincoln, Nebraska team in the Independent League.

Dan O'Brien

- January 7, 1976: Drafted by the St. Louis Cardinals in the 3rd round of the 1976 amateur draft (January Secondary).
- November 9, 1979: Purchased by the Seattle Mariners from the St. Louis Cardinals.

An All American at Florida State, O'Brien appeared in 13 games covering 29 innings for the team in parts of 1978 & 1979. Dan did not have much success in the bigs, ending his major league career in '79 with a 1-3 record and 5.90 ERA, all with the Cardinals.

After baseball Dan completed his masters in counseling at SIU in 1982-83, along with duties as recruiting coordinator and pitching coach for the Salukis until moving to Michigan State for the same position from 1988-1991. A similar role followed at Michigan from 1991 to 1995. Since 2006, Dan has been a volunteer coach with the Eastern Michigan University baseball team

Claude Osteen

- August 15, 1974: Traded by the Houston Astros to the St. Louis Cardinals for a player to be named later and Ron Selak (minors). The St. Louis Cardinals sent Dan Larson (October 14, 1974) to the Houston Astros to complete the trade.
- April 5, 1975: Released by the St. Louis Cardinals.

A dependable lefty who won 196 games over his 18-year career (and lost almost as many- 195), Osteen pitched in only eight games with the Cardinals in 1974 with a 0-2 record in 22 2/3 innings. Osteen had accomplished a great deal by the time he hooked up with the Cardinals: 3 All Star Games (1967, '70 & '73), 20 wins in 1969 & 1972 along with ten consecutive seasons with 12 or more wins (1964-73). After the Dodgers fell behind 2 games to none in the 1965 World Series, Osteen pitched a 5-hit shutout to help lead the team to a World Series title against Minnesota.

After one season as pitching coach in the Phillies minor leagues, Claude was awarded the pitching coach position for the Cardinals, which he held from 1977-1980. His coaching career lasted over twenty years with stints with Philadelphia, Texas and Los Angeles. He was later a scout and consultant for Arizona before retiring in 2009.

Lowell Palmer

- May 16, 1972: Signed as a Free Agent with the St. Louis Cardinals.
- September 18, 1972: Selected off waivers by the Cleveland Indians from the St. Louis Cardinals.

A 1st round draft choice by Philadelphia in 1966, Palmer became known as a character throughout his career. Allegedly Palmer was sent back to the minors from spring training after dating manager Gene Mauchs' daughter. During the 1972 off-season, Lowell was a private investigator. And those shades! Check out Topps baseball card # 252 from 1970; totally cool. Palmer was sensitive to light, so he wore sunglasses while on the mound.

His tenure with the Redbirds was short-lived, a 0-3 record in 16 games in 1972, 25 walks and 26 strikeouts. Arm problems cut short his colorful career. He left sporting a career 5-18 record and 5.29 ERA. After his major league career ended in 1974, Lowell continued playing the game in senior baseball and softball leagues.

Stan Papi

- June 8, 1973: Traded by the Houston Astros to the St. Louis Cardinals for Ray Busse.
- February 14, 1975: Traded by the St. Louis Cardinals to the Montreal Expos for Craig Caskey.

Papi, acquired for the ineffective Ray Busse, made the Cardinals opening day roster in 1974, based on his .300 spring training average. He appeared in only eight games, batting 1 for 4, before being sent to the minors. It would be 1977 before he reached the majors again with Montreal.

Papi is well-known in Boston, having been acquired from Montreal for flaky, but popular Bill Lee. The outside walls of Fenway Park were pained with the slogan "Who the Hell is Stan Papi?" Papi batted under .200 for the Sox in 1979 while Lee won 16 games with the Expos. Stan's 6 year career ended after the 1982 season with a career .213 mark.

Harry Parker

- June 8, 1965: Drafted by the St. Louis Cardinals in the 4th round of the 1965 amateur draft.
- October 18, 1971: Traded by the St. Louis Cardinals with Jim Beauchamp, Chip Coulter and Chuck Taylor to the New York Mets for Jim Bibby, Rich Folkers, Charlie Hudson and Art Shamsky.
- August 4, 1975: Selected off waivers by the St. Louis Cardinals from the New York Mets.
- April 7, 1976: Traded by the St. Louis Cardinals to the Cleveland Indians for Roric Harrison.

A Highland, Illinois native, Harry first appeared with the club in 1970 & 1971, appearing in 11 games and 27 innings. Parker was traded to the Mets, where, in 1973 he spot-started and relieved during their "You Gotta Believe" season. Harry was reacquired late in 1975, appearing in 14 games with a 6.27 ERA. His six year career ended with a 15-21 mark, 3.85 ERA and 12 saves.

Upon his retirement from the game the following year, Harry worked for the state of Virginia as a programmer. He passed away in May 2012 at the age of 64.

Daryl Patterson

- June 25, 1971: Purchased by the St. Louis Cardinals from the Oakland Athletics.
- October 21, 1971: Returned to the Oakland Athletics by the St. Louis Cardinals following previous purchase.

Patterson, a member of the 1968 World Champion Tigers, had a brief stay with the club in 1971 (13 games, 1 save, 2 starts). Daryl is probably best known for having his ear gnawed on by the Reds Pedro Borbon during a brawl in 1974. He regarded his time in St. Louis as being enjoyable and the fans as being quite knowledgeable. His major league career ended at the conclusion of the 1974 season, with a 11-9 mark, 4.09 ERA and 11 saves during his years in the game.

Upon retiring from baseball after the '74 season, Patterson went to work for Pacific Gas & Electric. In twenty years with the company, he rose from helper to chief inspector.

Orlando Pena

- June 15, 1973: Purchased by the St. Louis Cardinals from the Baltimore Orioles.
- September 5, 1974: Traded by the St. Louis Cardinals to the California Angels for a player to be named later. The California Angels sent Rich Hand (October 15, 1974) to the St. Louis Cardinals to complete the trade.

Pena, a likable reliever with an assortment of pitches was a valuable asset to the bullpen in 1973 & 74. With the exception of two seasons as starter for the KC A's (and 20 losses in 1963) Orlando was exclusively a relief pitcher. MVP of the Cuban League in 1958-59, Pena had a 9-6 record and 2.36 ERA with 7 saves during his time with the Redbirds in 1973 & '74 Called "Old Reliable" by long time St. Louis sportswriter Neal Russo, the 14 year major league veteran pitched into his mid 40's in the AAA Inter-American League in 1979. His major league ledger ended with a 56-77 record, 3.71 ERA and 40 saves.

An accomplished barber, Orlando often cut the hair of his fellow teammates. A member of the Cuban Hall of Fame (2000), Orlando has done some scouting in the Detroit organization.

Mike Phillips

- June 15, 1977: Traded by the New York Mets to the St. Louis Cardinals for Joel Youngblood.
- December 8, 1980: Traded by the St. Louis Cardinals with Terry Kennedy, John Littlefield, Al Olmsted, Kim Seaman, Steve Swisher and John Urrea to the San Diego Padres for a player to be named later, Rollie Fingers, Bob Shirley and Gene Tenace. The San Diego Padres sent Bob Geren (December 10, 1980) to the St. Louis Cardinals to complete the trade.

A first-round draft pick of the Giants in 1969, Phillips played from 1977-1980 with the Cardinals, batting a cumulative .246 during his time here. Mike enjoyed his best season with the Redbirds in 1978, appearing in 76 games while batting .268. A steady infielder, he hit for the cycle against the Cubs while playing for the Mets. He parlayed his hard work into an 11 season career, ending in 1983 with a career .240 average.

After baseball, Mike returned to his native Texas, where he was Director of Sports Marketing for a Dallas radio station from 1987-1995. He then moved into the Texas Rangers organization as Director of Corporate Sports from 1996-2000. Mike is currently Senior Director of Corporate and Group Sales with the Kansas City Royals.

Tim Plodinec

- June 7, 1968: Drafted by the St. Louis Cardinals in the 33rd round of the 1968 amateur draft.

Tim was a successful collegiate pitcher, helping to lead Team USA to a gold metal at the 1967 Pan American games. A proud member of the University of Arizona's Plaza Wall of Fame, Tim appeared in only 1 major league game, allowing 3 hits in 1/3 of an inning against the Dodgers in June 1972.

He reminisced, "My whole life growing up, all I wanted was to play pro ball. I dreamed of making it to the big leagues. I tell kids now that my dream wasn't big enough, I should have dreamed of making the Hall of Fame." Tim is now an accountant for a California seafood importer.

Mike Potter

- January 13, 1971: Drafted by the St. Louis Cardinals in the 6th round of the 1971 amateur draft (January Secondary).
- October 27, 1978: the St. Louis Cardinals sent Mike Potter to the Seattle Mariners to complete an earlier deal made on June 26, 1978.
- June 26, 1978: The St. Louis Cardinals sent a player to be named later to the Seattle Mariners for Jose Baez.

A .273 hitter and four seasons of 20 + home runs over 9 seasons in the minors, Mike could not find the mark in the majors. Brought up to the Cardinals in late 1976 & 77, Mike was hitless in 23 career at bats, including 8 strikeouts. Perhaps he needed his namesake Harry's magical spells to help him out. He never returned to the major leagues, ending his career in 1979.

Mike Proly

- June 6, 1972: Drafted by the St. Louis Cardinals in the 9th round of the 1972 amateur draft. Player signed June 10, 1972.
- December 6, 1976: Drafted by the Minnesota Twins from the St. Louis Cardinals in the 1976 rule 5 draft.
-

Starting his major league career with the Cardinals in 1976, Proly had a 1-0 record and 3.71 ERA over 17 innings. After being sent to AA Arkansas after the season, he was selected in the minor league draft. Mike played most of his seven year career with both Chicago teams, appearing in over 60 games in both 1980 and 1983. His major league career ended in 1983 with a career mark of 22-29 and 3.23 ERA.

Having earned his degree in marketing from St. Johns, Mike has been involved in financial services at Met Life for many years.

Dave Rader

- October 20, 1976: Traded by the San Francisco Giants with Mike Caldwell and John D'Acquisto to the St. Louis Cardinals for Willie Crawford, John Curtis and Vic Harris.
- December 8, 1977: Traded by the St. Louis Cardinals with Hector Cruz to the Chicago Cubs for Jerry Morales, Steve Swisher and cash.

The Sporting News Rookie of the Year in 1972 with the Giants, Rader enjoyed six seasons with the Giants, over half of them as a starting catcher including back-to-back .291 seasons. Radar saw limited duty with the Cardinals in 1977, especially playing behind the switch-hitting Simmons. He also had to leave the team two times to help care for his ailing wife. Dave batted .263 his only season with the club with 16 RBI's. Valuable coming off the bench that season, Dave was six out of nine in his first pinch-hitting appearances. Playing only 38 games at catcher, nearly half as a non-starter, Rader asked to be traded after the season.

He was the starter the next season with the Cubs but hit only 203 before closing out his career two seasons later in Boston, ending with a .257 career average.

Milt Ramirez

- December 1, 1969: Drafted by the St. Louis Cardinals from the Baltimore Orioles in the 1969 rule 5 draft.
- November 28, 1972: Traded by the St. Louis Cardinals with Skip Jutze to the Houston Astros for Ray Busse and Bobby Fenwick.

A 20-year old in his debut season with the Redbirds in 1970, Ramirez was a decent fielding, light hitting infielder, evidenced by his .190 average and 3 RBI's in 79 at bats that season. Milt was in 4 games with the Cards the following year before he was packaged in the deal to obtain Ray Busse as the shortstop of the future.

Ramirez bounced around the minor leagues another seven years before making a final big league appearance with Oakland in 1979, batting .161 in 28 games. His professional career ended the next season in the Mexican League, concluding his three year career in the majors with a .184 average and 28 hits.

Mike Ramsey

- June 3, 1975: Drafted by the St. Louis Cardinals in the 3rd round of the 1975 amateur draft.
- July 1, 1984: Traded by the St. Louis Cardinals to the Montreal Expos for Chris Speier and cash.

A utility infielder for the Redbirds six of his seven major seasons, Ramsey was a scrappy, good fielding infielder who averaged .245 during his run with the team. I will always remember him sliding into third base during the Cardinals comeback in the sixth inning of Game 7 of the 1982 World Series. Mike finished his career with the Dodgers in 1985.

Mike managed in the Cardinal minor leagues from 1992-'95 before taking managing positions in the Padres, Rays and Giants organizations, covering twelve seasons. He was named the Southern Leagues' Manager of the Year in 1998 with AA Mobile.

Eric Rasmussen

- June 5, 1973: Drafted by the St. Louis Cardinals in the 32nd round of the 1973 amateur draft.
- May 26, 1978: Traded by the St. Louis Cardinals to the San Diego Padres for George Hendrick.
- December 9, 1981: Purchased by the St. Louis Cardinals from Yucatan (Mexican).
- April 6, 1982: Purchased by Yucatan (Mexican) from the St. Louis Cardinals.
- August 11, 1982: Purchased by the St. Louis Cardinals from Yucatan (Mexican).
- August 2, 1983: Purchased by the Kansas City Royals from the St. Louis Cardinals.

Named Harold or Harry at birth, Rasmussen changed his name to Eric after the 1976 season. A starter exclusively during the Cardinals 1977 season, Rasmussen pitched in tough luck that 17 loss year. Three times the team was shut out, 6 times the team scored one run, and 4 times the Cards scored only two runs. His era during his first run with the team (1975-'78) was always consistently in the 3.50 range.

After three seasons in San Diego and two years in the Mexican League, Eric returned for a brief run with the World Champion team of 1982 (and 6 games with the club in 1983). He finished up his major league career in 1983 with a career 50-77 record and 3.94 ERA.

Rasmussen has remained in the game since then. Beginning his coaching career with a job in the Cleveland organization in 1988, Eric has worked in the Minnesota minor leagues since 1991 as a pitching coach at various levels. In 2009, he was appointed minor league pitching coordinator for the Twins. He also developed equitee, a batting device designed to produce a quick and correct swing.

Ron Reed

- May 28, 1975: Traded by the Atlanta Braves with a player to be named later to the St. Louis Cardinals for Ray Sadecki and Elias Sosa. The Atlanta Braves sent Wayne Nordhagen (June 2, 1975) to the St. Louis Cardinals to complete the trade.
- December 9, 1975: Traded by the St. Louis Cardinals to the Philadelphia Phillies for Mike Anderson.

One of only five pitchers to have 100 wins, 100 saves and 50 complete games, the two-sport athlete from Notre Dame also played two seasons with the NBA's Detroit Pistons, averaging 7 points a game, including a 30 point game. The 6'6" right-hander had a 9-8 record for the Redbirds in 1975 with a 3.23 ERA, which should have been better for lack of run support. An All Star with Atlanta in 1968, Reed was the starting and winning pitcher during Henry Aaron's record breaking 715 home run. Reed spent eight seasons in Philadelphia, helping the Phillies win the World Series in 1980. He ended his career in 1984 with 146 wins.

A member of the Indiana Baseball Hall of Fame (1990), Ron is the supervisor of an event management company in the Atlanta area, that organizes charitable events for organizations.

Ken Reitz

- June 5, 1969: Drafted by the St. Louis Cardinals in the 31st round of the 1969 amateur draft. Player signed July 14, 1969.
- December 8, 1975: Traded by the St. Louis Cardinals to the San Francisco Giants for Pete Falcone.
- December 10, 1976: Traded by the San Francisco Giants to the St. Louis Cardinals for Lynn McGlothen.
- December 9, 1980: Traded by the St. Louis Cardinals with a player to be named later and Leon Durham to the Chicago Cubs for Bruce Sutter. The St. Louis Cardinals sent Ty Waller (December 22, 1980) to the Chicago Cubs to complete the trade.
- July 21, 1983: Signed as a Free Agent with the St. Louis Cardinals.

The Zamboni enjoyed an 11 year career in the bigs, 8 of them with the Cardinals. A career .263 hitter with the team, Ken steadily improved his RBI's during his stay, reaching a high of 79 in 1979. A 1980 All Star and 1975 Gold Glove winner, Ken also lead third basemen in fielding percentage for 6 years.

After his trade to the Cubs in 1981, his career quickly spiraled due to his battles with drugs and alcohol. His career ended the following season with over 1200 career hits.

Life is good for Reitz these days. He was recently hired by former teammate Joe Torre, now the executive vice president of baseball operations for Major League Baseball. Ken monitors the major league game's progress, in addition to scouting duties and keeping up on his golf game!

Jerry Reuss

- June 6, 1967: Drafted by the St. Louis Cardinals in the 2nd round of the 1967 amateur draft.

- April 15, 1972: Traded by the <u>St. Louis Cardinals</u> to the <u>Houston Astros</u> for <u>Lance Clemons</u> and <u>Scipio Spinks</u>.

Another one who got away, Reuss was a Ritenour High School grad who won 220 games over his career, 198 of them by teams not named Cardinals! Making his debut in 1969, the 20 year old hurled a seven inning two-hitter, getting a base hit as well. After an uneven 14-14 record in 1971, Reuss, like fellow lefthander Carlton, was traded over

contract issues, or perhaps his mustache! Jerry went on to pitch in four different decades (like Tim McCarver), make the All Star Team in 1975 & 1980, win a World Series with the Dodgers in 1981, not to mention a no-hitter in 1980 and 12 seasons of 10+ wins.

After his pitching career ended, Jerry worked for ESPN as well as the Angels and Dodgers broadcasts. He returned to uniform as a pitching coach for the Montreal, Cubs and Mets minor leagues. Currently, Jerry broadcasts the Las Vegas minor league games, where he makes his home.

<u>Bob Reynolds</u>

- June 15, 1971: Traded by the <u>Montreal Expos</u> to the <u>St. Louis Cardinals</u> for <u>Mike Torrez</u>.
- July 29, 1971: Traded by the <u>St. Louis Cardinals</u> with <u>Jose Cardenal</u> and <u>Dick Schofield</u> to the <u>Milwaukee Brewers</u> for <u>Charlie Loseth</u> (minors) and <u>Ted Kubiak</u>.

"Bullet" Bob , a first round pick of the Giants in 1966; had a fastball that topped over 100 MPH. He pitched only four games with the Redbirds in 1971, allowing 15 hits and an ERA of 10.29 over 7 innings. Considering the length and success of Mike Torrez' career, this has to rank as another of the worst deals of the decade. Bob had success with the Orioles in 1973 & 74, winning 14 games and saving 16 (21 for his career) before his career ended in 1976, 34 days short of a major league pension.

After a season in Japan, Mexico and the Inter-American Leagues, Bob called in quits after 1979. Reynolds became a truck driver for 15 years and worked in security in the Seattle, Washington area.

Ken Reynolds

- October 2, 1973: Purchased by the St. Louis Cardinals from the Milwaukee Brewers.
- April 8, 1976: Traded by the St. Louis Cardinals with Bob Stewart (minors) to the San Diego Padres for Danny Frisella.

A three-sport athlete in high school, the lefty Reynolds could not parlay his success to the major leagues. A starting pitcher in 1971 & '72 for poor Philadelphia teams, Reynolds lost 12 straight games at the start of the 1972 season, resulting in a 2-15 record and 4.26 ERA. After overcoming elbow surgery in 1974, Reynolds was in 10 games for the Cards in 1975 with a 1.59 ERA in 17 innings. He hung around the minors until 1979 including a turn as player-coach, accumulating 118 wins, as opposed to his 7-29 major league record and 4.46 ERA.

Ken coached in the Cubs farm system for a few seasons before returning to his high school in Massachusetts, where he teaches physical education and coached the baseball team for a number of years. His teams won titles in 1982, '84, '86 and '87.

Lee "Bee Bee" Richard

- December 12, 1975: Traded by the Chicago White Sox to the St. Louis Cardinals for Buddy Bradford and Greg Terlecky.
- November 6, 1976: Released by the St. Louis Cardinals.

The White Sox first round pick in the 1970 draft, Lee earned his nickname in high school on the basis of the speed of his fastball- like a bb pellet. As an infielder with the Sox, he was called "The Juggler" by broadcaster Harry Carey for his defensive gaffs. With the Cardinals in 1976, not much changed. The starting shortstop on opening day, Bee Bee committed four errors in 12 games at short, an abysmal .857 fielding percentage. He ended the season batting .176 with 5 RBI's.

After a few seasons in the minors as well as the Mexican League and the Inter-American League in 1979, Bee Bee retired, batting .209 with 29 RBI's during his major league career.

Pete Richert

- December 5, 1973: Traded by the Los Angeles Dodgers to the St. Louis Cardinals for Tommie Agee.
- June 21, 1974: Purchased by the Philadelphia Phillies from the St. Louis Cardinals.

Moe Drabowski, Frank Bertania, Orlando Pena and now Pete Richert. The Cardinals of the early '70's seemed to be mimicking the birds from Baltimore by acquiring their former relief pitchers from their glory days of 1966-1971. Richert had begun his 13-year career as a starter with the Dodgers in 1962 in amazing fashion, striking out the first six batters he faced. He earned his first of two World Series rings with the club the following season. Pete later put together two consecutive All Star game appearances with Washington in 1965 & 66 before winning a World Series title with the other "birds" in 1970.

Pete was in his final major league season with the Cardinals, appearing in 13 games covering 11 1/3 innings in 1974. He finished with a solid 80-73 mark, 3.19 ERA and 51 saves during his run. He later served as pitching coach for the Oakland AAA organization in the late '80's as well as being named the Giants AAA team pitching coach in 2000.

Octavio "Cookie" Rojas

- October 7, 1969: Traded by the Philadelphia Phillies with Dick Allen and Jerry Johnson to the St. Louis Cardinals for Byron Browne, Curt Flood, Joe Hoerner and Tim McCarver. Curt Flood refused to report to his new team. The St. Louis Cardinals sent Willie Montanez (April 8, 1970) and Jim Browning (minors) (August 30, 1970) to the Philadelphia Phillies to complete the trade.
- June 13, 1970: Traded by the St. Louis Cardinals to the Kansas City Royals for Fred Rico.

Cookie Rojas batting average dropped precipitously over the past four years with the Phillies when the Redbirds acquired him in the infamous Curt Flood deal. With Julian Javier holding on to the starting second base job in 1970 based on a team leading batting average of .371 in spring training, Cookie sat. After a .106 average in only 47 at bats, Cookie was shipped across state to Kansas City where he appeared in four consecutive All Star games (1971-1974). He finished his 16 year career in 1977, ending with a .263 average and over 1600 hits.

A 16 year veteran, Cookie remained in baseball after retirement, coaching for the Mets, Blue Jays and Marlins, as well as manager of the Angels in 1988. A member of both the Phillies and Royals Hall of Fame (as well as the Cuban HOF), Cookie is currently the Spanish television color commentator for Miami Marlins baseball.

Jorge Roque

- Before 1967 Season: Signed by the St. Louis Cardinals as an amateur free agent.
- November 6, 1972: Traded by the St. Louis Cardinals to the Montreal Expos for Tim McCarver.

One of the great Cardinal names of the era, Roque hit .128 over parts of the 1970-72 season. After a horrid .061 average against right handers in '72, Roque was traded away. After a great winter league offseason, Jorge was installed as the rightfielder for the Expos in the '73 season. After two stints 2 for 24, he was sent back to the minors for good, performing in the minors and Mexican leagues through 1979. He finished with 19 career hits.

Ken Rudolph

- October 14, 1974: Traded by the San Francisco Giants with Elias Sosa to the St. Louis Cardinals for Marc Hill.
- March 31, 1977: Purchased by the San Francisco Giants from the St. Louis Cardinals.
- February 2, 1978: Signed as a Free Agent with the St. Louis Cardinals.

A solid defensive catcher, Rudolph was drafted in 1965 ahead of another future catcher (and Hall of Famer) Johnny Bench. Playing behind Ted Simmons in 1975 & '76, Ken had few opportunities with the club, appearing in 71 games during two seasons, batting .200 and .160 respectively. He concluded his nine-year career in 1977 with a career average of .213.

A member of the Cubs alumni association, Rudolph taught physical education and is the head baseball coach at a high school in Phoenix, Arizona. He also assists the Diamondbacks organization during the summer.

Ray Sadecki

- Before 1958 Season: Signed by the St. Louis Cardinals as an amateur free agent.
- May 8, 1966: Traded by the St. Louis Cardinals to the San Francisco Giants for Orlando Cepeda.

- October 13, 1974: Traded by the New York Mets with Tommy Moore to the St. Louis Cardinals for Joe Torre.
- May 28, 1975: Traded by the St. Louis Cardinals with Elias Sosa to the Atlanta Braves for a player to be named later and Ron Reed. The Atlanta Braves sent Wayne Nordhagen (June 2, 1975) to the St. Louis Cardinals to complete the trade.

Making his major league debut at 19 for the Redbirds in 1960 and Cardinal Rookie of the Year that season, Sadecki was a major contributor to the team's 1964 World Series title run. A twenty game winner that season, Sadecki won game one of the series against the New York Yankees. The lefty pitched eighteen seasons in the majors without missing a start or going on the disabled list.

A relief pitcher towards the end of his career, Ray was a big spark out of the bullpen for the Mets "You Gotta Believe" 1973 season. Reacquired by the Cards over the winter of 1974, Sadecki won his salary arbitration against the team, prompting his quick trade early in 1975, pitching only 11 innings with a 1-0 record in 8 games.

After retiring in 1977 with 135 wins and 20 career shutouts, Sadecki worked in sales for an office products company for 13 years before returning to baseball in 1990. A member of the National Polish American Sports Hall of Fame (along with Stan Musial); Ray coached in the Cubs organization from 1990-93 before becoming the Giants roving instructor the following season.

Al Santorini

- June 11, 1971: Traded by the San Diego Padres to the St. Louis Cardinals for Leron Lee and Fred Norman.
- May 8, 1973: Traded by the St. Louis Cardinals to the Kansas City Royals for Tom Murphy.

A first round draft pick of the Atlanta Braves in 1966, Santorini was already bothered by shoulder problems upon his acquisition by the

Cardinals in 1971. His best season for the club was 1972, where he compiled a 8-11 record with back-to back shutouts late in the season. His major league career ended the following season with a career mark of 17-38 and a 4.29 ERA over 6 seasons.

After retirement from baseball; Al picked up a variety of jobs- selling cars and real estate before making a career as a carpenter. He is now happily retired, living in New Jersey

Richie Scheinblum

- August 5, 1974: Purchased by the St. Louis Cardinals from the Kansas City Royals.

The only Jewish switch-hitter to bat .300 in a major league season, Scheinblum batted .263 over 8 seasons. After back-to-back .300+ seasons in 1972 & '73 (and a All Star spot in the former), Scheinblum hit a collective .183 in 1974; with the Redbirds he was 2 for 6 pinch-hitting. With the Cardinals having a number of young prospects for the '75 season, Richie was not added to the 40-man roster, ending his eight-year major league career.

Richie spent two seasons with Hiroshima in the Japan League before leaving the game for good after an Achilles injury. He later owned a jewelry store in California and recently worked at a company in Florida that makes corporate logos for businesses.

Dick Schofield

- June 3, 1953: Signed by the St. Louis Cardinals as an amateur free agent (bonus baby).
- June 15, 1958: Traded by the St. Louis Cardinals with cash to the Pittsburgh Pirates for Gene Freese and Johnny O'Brien.
- April 1, 1968: Signed as a Free Agent with the St. Louis Cardinals.

- December 3, 1968: Traded by the St. Louis Cardinals to the Boston Red Sox for Gary Waslewski.
- October 21, 1970: Traded by the Boston Red Sox to the St. Louis Cardinals for Jim Campbell.
- July 29, 1971: Traded by the St. Louis Cardinals with Jose Cardenal and Bob Reynolds to the Milwaukee Brewers for Charlie Loseth (minors) and Ted Kubiak.

"Ducky" began the first of his three go-rounds with the Cardinals in 1953 as an 18-year old infielder. A crucial reserve who filled in for an injured Dick Groat with the Pirates in 1960, Dick helped the team to a World Series title that season. The first batter in New York's Shea Stadium history, Schofield was reacquired by the Redbirds in 1968, almost earning himself another ring before the team's near miss against the Tigers. A .195 hitter over eight seasons with the team, he closed out his tenure with the club in 1971, ending his 19 seasons with a career .227 average.

Father of Dick, a shortstop primarily with the Angels in the 80's and 90's and grandfather of Jason Werth, (current slugger with the Nationals), Schofield served on the Springfield, Illinois Metropolitan Exposition and Auditorium Authority for over twenty years. He now enjoys gardening and golf in his retirement.

Charles "Buddy" Schultz

- February 28, 1977: Traded by the Chicago Cubs to the St. Louis Cardinals for Mark Covert (minors).

Buddy had an outstanding 1977 season with the Cardinals, a hard - throwing left hander out of the bullpen. He recorded a 6-1 record that season with a 2.32 ERA. He also started three games, receiving a standing ovation from the Busch Stadium crowd after leaving one of the games. Still effective in 1978, Buddy appeared in 62 games with six saves and a 3.80 ERA. 1979, his final season in the majors was plagued by injury, spending 67 days on the disabled list with tendinitis. After shoulder surgery, Buddy retired after attempting a comeback in

AA ball. His five-year run in the majors ended with a career 15-9 record, 3.68 ERA and 12 saves.

Striking out 26 in a nine inning game for Miami University (Ohio), Schultz was elected to the colleges' athletic Hall of Fame in 2010. Buddy has been involved in youth sports charity work in Arizona since 1993 as well as a charitable organization for East Cleveland baseball. His MVP Promotions have raised monies through charity events, auctions, and golf tournaments for Major League Baseball and Football Alumni Associations and Walt Disney World on Ice, to name as few.

Tony Scott

- November 6, 1976: Traded by the Montreal Expos with Steve Dunning and Pat Scanlon to the St. Louis Cardinals for Bill Greif, Sam Mejias and Angel Torres.
- June 7, 1981: Traded by the St. Louis Cardinals to the Houston Astros for Joaquin Andujar.

A speedy, solid glove man, Scott manned the outfield for parts of five seasons, from 1977-1981. Hitting a career high .291 in a season cut short by a ligament injury in 1977, Tony became a starter in 1979 and 1980. His 1979 season produced 68 RBI's and 37 stolen bases along with a .259 average, leading the league in triples before fading during the last months. The 1980 season was a disappointment when he dropped to 28 ribbies, even though he lead center fielders in fielding percentage.

Tony had a good 1981 season with Houston batting .293. He finished his 11 year career in Montreal in 1984 with a .249 career average. Tony has assisted with the Metropolitan Junior Baseball Leagues as an instructor/manager, encouraging African American youth back to baseball.

Kim Seaman

- December 5, 1978: Traded by the New York Mets with Tom Grieve to the St. Louis Cardinals for Pete Falcone.
- December 8, 1980: Traded by the St. Louis Cardinals with Terry Kennedy, John Littlefield, Al Olmsted, Mike Phillips, Steve Swisher and John Urrea to the San Diego Padres for a player to be named later, Rollie Fingers, Bob Shirley and Gene Tenace. The San Diego Padres sent Bob Geren (December 10, 1980) to the St. Louis Cardinals to complete the trade.

Appearing in 25 of his career 26 games in 1980, Seaman had more opportunities once Whitey Herzog came on board as the Redbirds manager. Kim recorded a 3-2 record, 3.42 ERA and 4 saves during the 1980 season. He was packaged in the huge trade in which Rollie Fingers was acquired until, of course, he was not. Kim toiled in the minors after that, retiring after the 1983 season.

Seaman is living in his hometown in Mississippi where he is involved in real estate.

Diego Segui

- June 7, 1972: Sent to the St. Louis Cardinals by the Oakland Athletics as part of a conditional deal.
- December 7, 1973: Traded by the St. Louis Cardinals with Reggie Cleveland and Terry Hughes to the Boston Red Sox for John Curtis, Mike Garman and Lynn McGlothen.

Segui appeared in 98 games with the club in 1972-73, having an excellent '73 season with a 7-6 record, 2.78 ERA and 17 saves, a career high. The only player to appear with both Seattle teams (the Pilots & Mariners), Segui started the Mariners inaugural game in 1977 at the age of 40, earning his title as "The Ancient Mariner" his last season in the majors. The 15 year veteran accumulated a career 92-111 record with a 3.81 ERA and 71 saves, 26 of those with the Redbirds. Diego also lead the league in ERA in 1970 with a 2.56 mark while pitching for Oakland. Father of ex-major leaguer David, Diego pitched in the Mexican League through the 1985 season (at the age of 47) hurling a no-hitter at the age of 40. He now lives on a farm not far from Kansas City, just down the road from his son.

Mike Shannon

- Before 1958 Season: Signed by the St. Louis Cardinals as an amateur free agent.

Shannon was an integral part of the Cardinals World Series titles in 1964 & 1967, hitting home runs in each series as well as in 1968. A starting right fielder at the beginning of his major league career in 1962, Mike moved to third base in 1967 to accommodate newly acquired Roger Maris. A career .255 hitter with good RBI numbers, Shannon's career was cut short by kidney disease in 1970. Mike joined the front office staff in 1971 and started his broadcasting career in 1972. In his 40 seasons as a member of the team's broadcast teams, Shannon has been a part of seven World Series seasons (1982, 1985, 1987, 2004, 2006, 2011 & 2013) and was awarded an Emmy in 1985 for his work. In addition to his immense charity work, Shannon owns an upscale restaurant that bears his name. He was also inducted into the Missouri Sports Hall of Fame in 1999.

Don Shaw

- May 19, 1970: Purchased by the St. Louis Cardinals from the Montreal Expos.
- May 15, 1972: Traded by the St. Louis Cardinals to the Oakland Athletics for Dwain Anderson.

Shaw, a left-hander out of the bullpen in 1971, had an excellent 7-2 record, 2.65 ERA in 45 games (with 2 saves). Winner of the first major league international game in 1969 (New York at Montreal) Shaw appeared in only 8 games with the club in 1972 before being dealt to

Oakland. His major league career ended soon after with a career 13-14 record, 4.01 ERA and 6 saves over his five year career.

After baseball, Shaw worked as an executive in sales and marketing in the insurance industry for over 25 years. Don holds both a insurance broker and real estate license.

Bob Shirley

- December 8, 1980: Traded by the San Diego Padres with a player to be named later, Rollie Fingers and Gene Tenace to the St. Louis Cardinals for Terry Kennedy, John Littlefield, Al Olmsted, Mike Phillips, Kim Seaman, Steve Swisher and John Urrea. The San Diego Padres sent Bob Geren (December 10, 1980) to the St. Louis Cardinals to complete the trade.
- April 1, 1982: Traded by the St. Louis Cardinals to the Cincinnati Reds for Jose Brito (minors) and Jeff Lahti.

An Oklahoma City native, Shirley starred in high school with his battery mate, future NFL Hall of Famer Steve Largent. A left-handed starter, swingman and reliever at parts of his career, Shirley made his major league debut month in 1977 a great one. Bob struck out 11 in his first major league start, then retired the first 25 batters he faced against the Astros shortly thereafter. He lead the Padres in wins that season with 12. In his only season with the Cardinals in 1981, Shirley enjoyed his only full season with a winning record, recording a 6-4 record, 4.08 ERA and 11 starts in 28 games covering 79 1/3 Innings. Noted Shirley, "Tradition in St. Louis is Stan Musial coming into the clubhouse and making the rounds, tradition in San Diego is Nate Colbert coming into the clubhouse and trying to sell you a used car." Having a horrible spring training in the 1982 championship season, Bob was traded before the season opened.

His major league career lasted eleven seasons, ending in 1987 with a 67-94 record and 3.82 ERA. Bob later managed, then coached for a short time in the Blue Jays minor leagues.

Wilfred "Sonny" Siebert

- October 26, 1973: Traded by the Texas Rangers to the St. Louis Cardinals for Tommy Cruz and cash.
- November 18, 1974: Traded by the St. Louis Cardinals with Rich Folkers and Alan Foster to the San Diego Padres for a player to be named later and Ed Brinkman. The San Diego Padres sent Danny Breeden (December 10, 1974) to the St. Louis Cardinals to complete the trade.

A St. Mary, Missouri native and Bayless High School grad, Sonny had an eight-year run with 10 or more victories each season from 1965-72. A two-time All Star (1966 & 1971) with a no hitter to his credit, Sonny arrived in St. Louis at the age of 37. Siebert began his Cardinal tenure with a shutout in his first start before age and injuries caught up with him. He finished with an 8-8 record, 3.84 ERA and 3 shutouts that season.

After a career that lasted 12 years, Sonny called it quits after the following season, ending up with 140 wins against 114 losses, a 3.21 ERA and 21 career shutouts. After owning and operating an ice cream store and newspaper routes, Siebert returned to the game in 1984. Sonny worked in the San Diego organization as a pitching instructor in every level of the organization, including 1994 & '95 as the Padres pitching coach. He now enjoys retirement in the St. Louis area.

Ted Simmons

- June 6, 1967: Drafted by the St. Louis Cardinals in the 1st round (10th pick) of the 1967 amateur draft.
- December 12, 1980: Traded by the St. Louis Cardinals with Rollie Fingers and Pete Vuckovich to the Milwaukee Brewers for David Green, Dave LaPoint, Sixto Lezcano and Lary Sorensen.

"Simba", was a career .298 hitter for the Redbirds during his tenure with the team from 1968-1980. Simmons has to be regarded as the best catcher in baseball not in the Hall of Fame. He has more RBI's than Johnny Bench, more hits than Yogi Berra or Carlton Fisk, but no plaque. Owner of 2,472 career hits, the switch-hitting catcher was a 5-time All Star with the club in the 70's, highlighted by his lone starting role in 1978. Highly competitive, Ted was involved in confrontations with friend (teammate John Denny) and foe alike (Bill Madlock, Cubs).

His 21-year career ended with Atlanta in 1988, with a .285 average, 2,472 hits, 248 homers and 1389 RBI's. Ted was involved in player development with the Cardinals until 1992 when he became general manager of the Pittsburgh Pirates. Upon leaving that position due to a heart attack, Simmons toiled in the front office/scout positions with Cleveland and San Diego. He was hired as senior advisor to the G.M. position of the Seattle Mariners in 2010.

Ted Sizemore

- October 5, 1970: Traded by the <u>Los Angeles Dodgers</u> with <u>Bob Stinson</u> to the <u>St. Louis Cardinals</u> for <u>Dick Allen</u>.
- March 2, 1976: Traded by the <u>St. Louis Cardinals</u> to the <u>Los Angeles Dodgers</u> for <u>Willie Crawford</u>.

Sizemore, a career .260 hitter with the Redbirds over 5 seasons, was a solid number two-hitter who greatly contributed to Lou Brocks' record-setting stolen base record in 1974. Said Brock, "You have to have the right man hitting behind you, I do, Ted Sizemore." Rookie of the Year in 1969 with the Dodgers, Ted enjoyed a 12-year career in the majors before retiring after the 1980 season in Boston with a career .262 average and over 1300 hits.

Today, Ted is an executive at Rawlings Sporting Goods, in charge of supplying major league baseball with most of its equipment. He also has devoted time being on the board of directors for both the Cystic Fibrosis Foundation as well as the Baseball Assistance Program.

Keith Smith

- January 12, 1972: Drafted by the St. Louis Cardinals in the 7th round of the 1972 amateur draft (January), but did not sign.
- June 6, 1972: Drafted by the Texas Rangers in the 4th round of the 1972 amateur draft (June Secondary).
- February 12, 1979: Traded by the Texas Rangers to the St. Louis Cardinals for Tommy Toms.

A nine-year minor league veteran, Smith had his best opportunity in 1977 with Texas, batting .239 in 67 at bats. A career .295 minor league hitter, Keith had limited opportunities with the Redbirds in 1979 & '80, appearing in only 30 games and batting a cumulative .159 in 41 at bats with 7 hits. His professional career ended in the minor leagues in 1981.

Reggie Smith

- October 26, 1973: Traded by the Boston Red Sox with Ken Tatum to the St. Louis Cardinals for Bernie Carbo and Rick Wise.
- June 15, 1976: Traded by the St. Louis Cardinals to the Los Angeles Dodgers for Fred Tisdale (minors), Bob Detherage and Joe Ferguson.

A five-tool player (hits for power & average, good glove and arm plus speed) for the team from 1974 to mid '76, Reggie was especially good in his first season with the Cards, batting .309 with 23 home runs and 100 RBI's. A seven time All Star, Reggie batted .293 during his time with the team. After a slight dropoff in 1975 in RBI's (76), Reggie, along with the team, struggled early in 1976. Less than a month after hitting three home runs in a game (the first Cardinal to do so since Stan the Man), he was traded in another confounding deal for a catcher they did not even need, Joe Ferguson. Ferguson was traded at the end of the 1976 season.

Smith played another six years, earning a World Series Ring in 1981 and leaving with a career .287 average, over 2000 hits and 314 home runs. Reggie was later the minor league field coordinator for the Dodgers organization before becoming the team's batting coach from 1994-1999. He has run a youth baseball camp since 1995 and since 1998, the Reggie Smith Baseball Center, a facility for players of all ages.

Eddie Solomon

- July 22, 1975: Traded by the <u>Chicago Cubs</u> to the <u>St. Louis Cardinals</u> for <u>Ken Crosby</u>.
- May 24, 1977: Purchased by the <u>Atlanta Braves</u> from the <u>St. Louis Cardinals</u>.

A highly regarded talent when drafted by the Dodgers, Solomon was brought up from Tulsa in June 1976. In his half season with the Redbirds Solomon appeared in 26 games covering 37 innings, including two starts with a 1-1 record and 4.86 ERA. A spot starter most of his career, Eddie had his best seasons with Pittsburgh, recording a 7-3 record and 2.69 ERA in 1980 and 8-6, 3.12 the following season. His ten year tenure in the majors ended in 1982 with a career 36-42 mark and 4.00 ERA.

Solomon was an auto salesman in Macon, Georgia after baseball. He perished in January 1986 in a single car accident in Macon at the age of 34.

Elias Sosa

- October 14, 1974: Traded by the San Francisco Giants with Ken Rudolph to the St. Louis Cardinals for Marc Hill.
- May 28, 1975: Traded by the St. Louis Cardinals with Ray Sadecki to the Atlanta Braves for a player to be named later and Ron Reed. The Atlanta Braves sent Wayne Nordhagen (June 2, 1975) to the St. Louis Cardinals to complete the trade.

Sosa will probably be recognized as one of the three Dodger pitchers to give up a home run in Reggie Jackson's epic 1977 World Series game. He enjoyed a number of very good years in his 12 year career out of the bullpen with 59 wins, a 3.32 ERA and 83 saves. With the Cardinals in 1975, his stay was brief-14 games, one of his three career starts, a 0-3 record, 3.97 ERA before heading to one of the other seven teams he would play for.

After leaving the majors in 1983, Elias played in the Mexican and Dominican leagues until securing a position with Major League Baseball. Elias is the special envoy for Latin American countries, providing seminars and clinics for coaches and youth in the hopes of spreading baseball's goodwill.

Ed Sprague

- Before 1966 Season: Signed by the St. Louis Cardinals as an amateur free agent.
- November 28, 1967: Drafted by the Oakland Athletics from the St. Louis Cardinals in the 1967 rule 5 draft.
- July 27, 1973: Traded by the Cincinnati Reds with a player to be named later to the St. Louis Cardinals for Gene Dusen (minors) and Ed Crosby. The Cincinnati Reds sent Roe Skidmore (September 30, 1973) to the St. Louis Cardinals to complete the trade.

- September 4, 1973: Purchased by the <u>Milwaukee Brewers</u> from the <u>St. Louis Cardinals</u>.

Sprague, signed by the club in 1966, appeared in 8 games covering 8 innings in 1973 with a 2.25 ERA. He was quickly dealt to Milwaukee near the end of the season, where he finished his career in 1976, ending parts of eight seasons in the majors with a 17-23 record, 3.84 ERA and nine saves. Ed's namesake was an 11-year veteran who won a couple World Series rings with the Blue Jays in the early 1990's. Ed was at one time owner of his hometown Stockton Ports Single A club. Because legend has it that the poem "Casey At The Bat" is based in Stockton, Ed outfitted the team with uniforms reading "Mudville." He later scouted for the Baltimore organization.

<u>Scipio Spinks</u>

- April 15, 1972: Traded by the <u>Houston Astros</u> with <u>Lance Clemons</u> to the <u>St. Louis Cardinals</u> for <u>Jerry Reuss</u>.
- March 23, 1974: Traded by the <u>St. Louis Cardinals</u> to the <u>Chicago Cubs</u> for <u>Jim Hickman</u>.

An effervescent, humorous addition to the club, Spinks was acquired during one of the Cardinals "spite" deals. Along with his "teammate and roommate," a stuffed gorilla named Mighty Joe Young, Scipio would bring the gorilla on road trips as well as in the Cardinal locker room. Clad in a batboy-sized uniform, Mighty Joe Young would accompany Scipio to television appearances and hospital visits.

On July 4th, 1972, Spinks career took a downward turn. Sliding into Johnny Bench on a play at home, Scipio tore ligaments in his knee which ended his season. I can still picture him hobbling away from the collision. Shoulder problems limited him to 8 games the following season and one more career victory, ending his major league career at 7-11 with a 3.70 ERA. Mighty Joe was sent to former teammate Bernie Carbo in Boston for safekeeping.

Upon retirement from the game as a player in 1975, Spinks has scouted and coached for the Houston and San Diego organizations. He now lives in Houston where he is involved in youth baseball programs.

Bill Stein

- June 5, 1969: Drafted by the St. Louis Cardinals in the 4th round of the 1969 amateur draft.
- September 25, 1973: Traded by the St. Louis Cardinals to the California Angels for Jerry DaVanon.

Drafted by the Cardinals in 1969, Stein batted .256 for the team in 90 at bats during brief appearances in 1972/73. He went on to enjoy a 14-year career with Chicago, Seattle and Texas, sporting a career .267 average. A starter for the expansion 1977 Seattle Mariners, Stein played every position in the major leagues except for pitcher, catcher and center field.

Upon his retirement in 1985, Bill managed from 1988-1994 in the Mets and Giants organization. He is now retired and living in Texas.

Bob Stinson

- October 5, 1970: Traded by the Los Angeles Dodgers with Ted Sizemore to the St. Louis Cardinals for Dick Allen.
- November 3, 1971: Traded by the St. Louis Cardinals to the Houston Astros for Marty Martinez.

With Ted Simmons and supersub Jerry McNertney in front of him, Stinson had little playing time in his only season with the team in 1971. A .211 average based on 4 hits and 1 RBI, Stinson enjoyed greater success later in his career with Montreal, Kansas City, and Seattle. An original Seattle Mariner, Bob ended his 12-year career with the club in 1980 with a career .250 average.

Bob stayed in the Seattle area for a number of years, working in landscaping and at the Boeing Corporation. He now lives in Orlando, Florida where he is a baseball and golf instructor.

Gary Sutherland

- January 3, 1978: Signed as a Free Agent with the St. Louis Cardinals.
- May 26, 1978: Released by the St. Louis Cardinals.

One of the original Montreal Expos, Sutherland played for the Cardinals one month before getting his release in 1978 after going one for six. Gary scored the first run in Expos history as well as recorded the first out on Canadian soil during a major league game, catching a line drive off the bat of Lou Brock. His best seasons were in Detroit in the mid seventies, where he lead the team in hits in 1974 with 157. His thirteen-year career ended with a .243 average.

Gary was briefly a real estate broker before returning to baseball as a scout for San Diego. It was his recommendation that the club sign eventual Hall of Famer Tony Gwynn. He also worked in the Cleveland and Dodger organizations before becoming the Angels scouting coordinator in 1999 and, eventually, a special assistant to the General Manager through the 2011 season.

Johnny Sutton

- October 22, 1976: Traded by the Texas Rangers to the St. Louis Cardinals for Mike Wallace.
- December 5, 1977: Drafted by the Minnesota Twins from the St. Louis Cardinals in the 1977 rule 5 draft.

Making the 1977 opening day roster along with John Urrea, Sutton pitched in 14 games covering 24 1/3 innings with a 2-1 record and 2.59 ERA before being sent down to AA New Orleans . Disenchanted with his demotion, Johnny was picked up by the Twins during the offseason, where he pitched in 17 games the following season with a 3.45 ERA.

Johnny stayed in baseball until 1985 including three seasons in the Mexican League. He never reached the majors again.

Steve Swisher

- December 8, 1977: Traded by the Chicago Cubs with Jerry Morales and cash to the St. Louis Cardinals for Hector Cruz and Dave Rader.
- December 8, 1980: Traded by the St. Louis Cardinals with Terry Kennedy, John Littlefield, Al Olmsted, Mike Phillips, Kim Seaman and John Urrea to the San Diego Padres for a player to be named later, Rollie Fingers, Bob Shirley and Gene Tenace. The San Diego Padres sent Bob Geren (December 10, 1980) to the St. Louis Cardinals to complete the trade.

Even though we are Cardinal fans (unlike the Cubs for example), we still have suffered heartache. The seventh game of the 1968 World Series, the sixth game of the 1985 Series, to name a few. Another was in October 1974, last game of the season, Cubs and Pirates. If the Cubs win, the Redbirds makeup a rainout, if they win that , they face the Bucs in a one game playoff. Cubs leading Pirates, two outs in the ninth, strike three! Cub catcher Steve Swisher cannot hold on to the pitch; the tying run scores. Bucs win in extra innings!

Four seasons later, Swisher came to the Cardinals for three seasons. He batted a career-best .278 in 115 at bats in 1978, but with work-horse Ted Simmons behind the plate, Swisher received limited opportunities. He wrapped up his nine-year career in 1982 with a .216 average.

After briefly selling cars after retirement, Steve became bullpen catcher for Cleveland before managing ten seasons in the minor leagues along with a stint on the Mets coaching staff from 1993-1996. He was named Manager of the Year for his efforts for Binghampton in 1992. He later became regional sales manager of a aluminum company. In 2010 Steve and his son Nick, a major leaguer now with Cleveland, were honored with a plaque in their native Parkersburg, West Virginia.

Bob Sykes

- December 4, 1978: Traded by the Detroit Tigers with Jack Murphy (minors) to the St. Louis Cardinals for Aurelio Lopez and Jerry Morales.
- October 21, 1981: Traded by the St. Louis Cardinals to the New York Yankees for Willie McGee.

Getting his chance with the Tigers when Mark "The Bird" Fidrych was injured, Sykes spot-started and relieved during his five-year career. Sykes hurled shutouts in the first two games he pitched in 1978. A blood clot in his arm limited him to 13 games with the Cardinals in 1979 with a 4-3 record and 6.18 ERA. Bob tossed three shutouts in 1980 in an otherwise mediocre 6-10 season. He was hardly used in the first half of the strike-ridden 1981 season however, his 1.90 ERA in the second half was the teams best.

In a trade that ranks as one of their best, Sykes was dispatched to the Yankees for a minor league outfielder named Willie McGee, who helped the club to three pennants during the '80's as well as earning the 1985 MVP. Bob never pitched in the majors again. The Cards later had to appease George Steinbrenner's claim of "damaged goods" by sending prospects Bobby Meacham and Stan Javier to the Yankees for three minor leaguers.

Sykes, a long time resident of Carmi, Illinois, worked 22 years at Tarton Oil Company before becoming a Deputy Sheriff in White County (IL) and teaching youth the dangers of substance abuse. He also operated "The Ballyard," an instructional baseball camp for youth.

John Tamargo

- June 5, 1973: Drafted by the St. Louis Cardinals in the 6th round of the 1973 amateur draft.
- July 18, 1978: Traded by the St. Louis Cardinals to the San Francisco Giants for a player to be named later. The San Francisco Giants sent Rob Dressler (July 24, 1978) to the St. Louis Cardinals to complete the trade.

Appearing in 20 games over parts of three seasons with the Cards, Tamargo batted .150 with 1 RBI before getting more opportunities with the Giants and later, Montreal. A career backup catcher, 1978 was the only one of his 5-year career in which he batted over 100 times. The 1980 season with Montreal was his last, ending up with a career .242 average, 4 homers and 33 RBI's.

It is said that the catcher is the field general of the team, and John exemplified that after his playing days. Tamargo has enjoyed over thirty years in baseball after his career ended, managing in the Mets, Astros, Brewers, and Mariners organizations. Under his leadership, he won the Eastern League Championship in 1994 with the Mets affiliate and the AAA World Series in 1998 with the Astros minor league team. John was also a coach with the parent Astros team from 1999-2004. He currently is the Latin American Field Coordinator for the Mariners organization.

Carl Taylor

- October 21, 1969: Traded by the Pittsburgh Pirates with Frank Vanzin (minors) to the St. Louis Cardinals for Dave Giusti and Dave Ricketts.
- October 20, 1970: Traded by the St. Louis Cardinals with Jim Ellis to the Milwaukee Brewers for Jesse Huggins (minors), George Lauzerique and Jerry McNertney.

After a career-high .348 in reserve duty with the Pirates in 1969, Taylor dropped to .249 in his only season with the Cards. Despite the drop in average, Taylor reached career highs in homers with 6 and RBI's with 45. On August 11, 1970, Carl became one of only 23 big leaguers to end a game with a walk-off grand slam. Roger Freed in 1979 was the only other Redbird to duplicate that feat.

After the poor '70 season, Carl was one of the 45% of the 40 man roster to be traded, in spite of finishing 2nd on the club in clutch hitting ratings. His major league career ended after his 1973 season with a .266 cumulative average and 225 hits.

Carl later worked for the Yankees in the 1990's as bullpen coach, video coordinator and resident barber, earning a World Series ring in 1996.

Chuck Taylor

- Before 1961 Season: Signed by the St. Louis Cardinals as an amateur free agent.
- February 17, 1964: Traded by the St. Louis Cardinals with Jim Beauchamp to the Houston Colt .45's for Carl Warwick.
- June 15, 1965: Traded by the Houston Astros with Hal Woodeshick to the St. Louis Cardinals for Mike Cuellar and Ron Taylor.

- October 18, 1971: Traded by the St. Louis Cardinals with Jim Beauchamp, Chip Coulter and Harry Parker to the New York Mets for Jim Bibby, Rich Folkers, Charlie Hudson and Art Shamsky.

Taylor was called up to the Cardinals in 1969 after eight seasons in the minors. A spot starter and reliever with the club from 1969-71, Chuck compiled a 16-13 record and solid 2.99 ERA. Chuck's greatest success came in 1974 with the Expos, appearing in 61 games with a 2.17 ERA and 11 saves. His career wound down after the 1976 season with a final mark of 28-20, a 3.07 ERA and 31 career saves.

Upon his exit from the game, Taylor has lived in his hometown of Murfreesboro, TN. Chuck has been associated with the Middle Tennessee State golf tournament which raises money for the baseball team, of which Chuck was a former member.

Garry Templeton

- June 5, 1974: Drafted by the St. Louis Cardinals in the 1st round (13th pick) of the 1974 amateur draft.
- December 10, 1981: Traded by the St. Louis Cardinals with a player to be named later and Sixto Lezcano to the San Diego Padres for a player to be named later, Steve Mura and Ozzie Smith. The San Diego Padres sent Al Olmsted (February 19, 1982) to the St. Louis Cardinals to complete the trade. The St. Louis Cardinals sent Luis DeLeon (February 19, 1982) to the San Diego Padres to complete the trade.

'Jump Steady' was one of the most dynamic hitting shortstops in Cardinal history. He was an All Star in two of his first three full seasons, a .300 hitter in three of his first four, the first switch hitter to get 100 hits from each side of the plate, along with leading the league in triples three consecutive years. He had good range, even though he lead the league in errors three consecutive years.

However, all good things.....during a 1981 "ladies day" game, Garry neglected to run out a strikeout that got away from the catcher, the crowd booed, Garry responded with the"bird"along with another gesture before being pulled into the dugout by manager Whitey Herzog. He was traded at the end of the season, ending his six year run with a .305 average (and the Redbirds getting Ozzie Smith in the process).

Garry was one of the emotional leaders on the '84 Padre team that went to the World Series, playing with the team for a decade before one season with the Mets in 1991. He ended with a .271 average over 2000 hits and over 200 stolen bases.

Templeton has managed in the minors since 1998, primarily in the independent leagues. As of 2013, he is the manager for the Newark Bears.

Greg Terlecky

- June 4, 1970: Drafted by the St. Louis Cardinals in the 5th round of the 1970 amateur draft.
- December 12, 1975: Traded by the St. Louis Cardinals with Buddy Bradford to the Chicago White Sox for Lee Richard.

Terlecky saw his only major league action in 1975, when he was briefly called up from Tulsa (and Keith Hernandez was briefly sent down). His stay consisted of 20 games covering 30 1/3 innings, he left with a 0-1 record and 4.45 ERA. He ended his nine year professional career with a season in the Mexican League in 1980. Greg won 67 games in the minor leagues.

For the past 25+ years, Greg has been a financial planner. He currently is the regional managing director of the Southern California Center of the Principal Financial Group. Not sure what that is, but it sounds more financially rewarding than his baseball career was!

Roy Thomas

- June 23, 1978: Selected off waivers by the St. Louis Cardinals from the Houston Astros.
- December 8, 1980: Drafted by the Oakland Athletics from the St. Louis Cardinals in the 1980 rule 5 draft.

Thomas was a versatile pitcher for the club in parts of three seasons with the club. Roy received his first major league victory in his first appearance with the team in 1978, pitching two innings against Pittsburgh to earn the win. The following season with a number of doubleheaders lurking (remember those?), Roy hurled a three hitter in a start covering 7 1/3 innings. He left the Redbirds after 1980 eventually winding up in Seattle, where in 1985 he recorded a sparkling 7-0 record, 3.36 ERA over 40 appearances.

Pitching parts of 16 seasons in the minor leagues along with parts of eight in the bigs, Roy hung them up after the 1990 season with a career record of 20-11, 3.82 ERA and 7 saves.

Taking college courses throughout his career, Roy earned his Masters in teaching certification in the '90's and is a middle school science and math teacher in the state of Washington. He also coaches the basketball team and JV baseball teams.

Mike Thompson

- March 31, 1973: the Texas Rangers sent Mike Thompson to the St. Louis Cardinals to complete an earlier deal made on February 1, 1973.
- February 1, 1973: The Texas Rangers sent a player to be named later to the St. Louis Cardinals for a player to be named later and Charlie Hudson.
- September 10, 1974: Purchased by the Atlanta Braves from the St. Louis Cardinals.

A hard-throwing right-hander, Thompson had a short stay in the majors. Wildness was his undoing. Making the opening day roster for the Cardinals in 1974, Thompson was moved to the bullpen after encountering control problems. Mike had a good if short run out of the pen, at one point not yielding a run for 11 innings over 8 appearances. A bartender in the off-season during his playing days, Thompson ended his major league stay in 1975 with a 1-15 career record and 4.86 ERA .

Joe Torre

- March 17, 1969: Traded by the Atlanta Braves to the St. Louis Cardinals for Orlando Cepeda.
- October 13, 1974: Traded by the St. Louis Cardinals to the New York Mets for Tommy Moore and Ray Sadecki.

Torre, a future Hall of Famer as manager of the late 1990's Yankee dynasty, was an excellent performer for the Cardinals during his 6-year run with the team. A .308 hitter with the team, Joe was named 1971 MVP based on his .363 average and 137 RBI's. A 4-time All Star with the team, Joe also enjoyed 3 consecutive 100 RBI seasons. With his trade to the Mets after the 1974 season, Joe had the unusual distinction of being traded full circle. The Cards traded Ray  Sedecki for Orlando Cepeda in 1966, traded Cepeda for Torre in 1969, and traded Torre for Sedecki in 1974. His eighteen-year major league career ended with a lifetime .297 average, 2342 hits and 252 dingers.

At the conclusion of his career in 1977, Joe managed the Braves, Cardinals (1990-1995, all during a tight budget), Yankees (1996-2007 with 4 World Series titles) and later the Dodgers, retiring after the 2010 season. Joe was appointed executive vice president for Baseball Operations in 2011, overseeing on-field operations, discipline, and umpires.

Mike Torrez

- September 10, 1964: Signed by the St. Louis Cardinals as an amateur free agent.
- June 15, 1971: Traded by the St. Louis Cardinals to the Montreal Expos for Bob Reynolds.

A wild, hard-throwing righthander, Torrez made his first major league appearance with the Cards in 1967. After a solid 10-4 record in 15 starts in 1969, Torrez regressed the following season (8-10 4.22 ERA) and was sent to Montreal in early 1971. A winner of 185 games in the majors, Torrez won more than 15 games for 6 consecutive seasons, all with 5 different teams. Winner of two games in the 1977 World Series with the  Champion Yankees, Torrez is famous for giving up the home run to Bucky "bleeping" Dent in the 1978 divisional playoff game while with the Red Sox. He ended with a career 185-160 mark with a 3.96 ERA.

Mike is now president of MAT premiums, a company that makes promotional items for businesses. He also previously served as general manager for the Newark Bears minor league team. In 2008, Torrez was inducted into the Kansas Baseball Hall of Fame.

Mike Tyson

- January 17, 1970: Drafted by the St. Louis Cardinals in the 3rd round of the 1970 amateur draft (January).
- October 17, 1979: Traded by the St. Louis Cardinals to the Chicago Cubs for Donnie Moore.

Mike, a career .244 hitter in 8 seasons with the Cardinals, was a lifesaver for the club in 1973; replacing a shaky Ray Busse at shortstop to almost lead the club to a division title. Cardinal Rookie of the year that season, Tyson had a career-high .286 average in 1976 and 6 RBI's in one game in August 1977. Eventually moving to second base, Mike was displaced by Ken Oberkfell and sent to Chicago at the conclusion of the '79 season.

Mike had two mediocre seasons with the Cubs and was released early in 1982, along with teammate Ken Reitz, due to another of the Cubs youth movements, ending with a career .241 average over 10 seasons.

Tom Underwood

- June 15, 1977: Traded by the Philadelphia Phillies with Rick Bosetti and Dane Iorg to the St. Louis Cardinals for Bake McBride and Steve Waterbury.
- December 6, 1977: Traded by the St. Louis Cardinals with Victor Cruz to the Toronto Blue Jays for a player to be named later and Pete Vuckovich. The Toronto Blue Jays sent John Scott (December 16, 1977) to the St. Louis Cardinals to complete the trade.

Underwood had early success in the majors with Philadelphia, especially in 1976, where he went 10-5 for the division winners. After being shuttled to the pen, Tom was acquired by the Redbirds to add a southpaw to their rotation. It did not last. Underwood ended up back in the bullpen, ending his season and his tenure with the Cardinals at 6-9 with a 4.95 ERA.

His trade to the Blue Jays was the first ever between two breweries, Anheuser-Busch and Labatts. In 1979, Tom pitched against his younger brother Pat in his major league debut. Even though Tom pitched a complete game, younger bro Pat got the victory.

His 11 year career ended in 1984 with 86 wins against 87 losses and four double-digit victory seasons. A member of the Indiana Baseball Hall of Fame (1997), Underwood became a financial advisor with Wells Fargo upon retirement. He died of pancreatic cancer in 2010 at the age of 56.

John Urrea

- January 9, 1974: Drafted by the St. Louis Cardinals in the 1st round (14th pick) of the 1974 amateur draft (January).
- December 8, 1980: Traded by the St. Louis Cardinals with Terry Kennedy, John Littlefield, Al Olmsted, Mike Phillips, Kim Seaman and Steve Swisher to the San Diego Padres for a player to be named later, Rollie Fingers, Bob Shirley and Gene Tenace. The San Diego Padres sent Bob Geren (December 10, 1980) to the St. Louis Cardinals to complete the trade.

A Cardinal first round draft pick in 1974, John made the 1977 opening day roster out of the bullpen. He got off to a great start too, the only Cardinal to earn saves in his first three relief appearances. The bad news is he earned only six more saves in his 4+ year career. He moved into the starting rotation that season with the club winning all of his first seven starts. He ended the season 7-6, 3.16 ERA 4 saves and 1 shutout, good for second in the Sporting News NL Rookie Pitcher of the Year. The following season John was moved back to the bullpen for good after going 2 months without a win. Urrea had a decent season in 1980 going 4-1 with a 3.48 ERA and 3 saves before being sent to San Diego after the season.

Urrea pitched one season with the Padres, recording a career-best 2.39 ERA before playing in Mexico in 1982 and 1986. He played in the 1990 Senior League before the organization dissolved. He finished his 5 year major league career at 17-18, a 3.74 ERA and 9 saves.

Bill Voss

- August 27, 1972: Traded by the Oakland Athletics with Steve Easton (minors) to the St. Louis Cardinals for Matty Alou.
- November 28, 1972: Traded by the St. Louis Cardinals to the Cincinnati Reds for Pat Jacquez

A short- lived member of the World Series Champion Oakland A's of 1972, Voss ended his 8 year major league career with the Cardinals with 4 hits in 15 at bats and 3 RBI's. Bill enjoyed his best season in 1969 with the Angels, batting .261 with 40 RBI's. Bill broke up Minnesota Twin Dean Chance's no-hit bid with one out in the ninth while with the White Sox in 1968

Pete Vuckovich

- December 6, 1977: Traded by the Toronto Blue Jays with a player to be named later to the St. Louis Cardinals for Victor Cruz and Tom Underwood. The Toronto Blue Jays sent John Scott (December 16, 1977) to the St. Louis Cardinals to complete the trade.
- December 12, 1980: Traded by the St. Louis Cardinals with Rollie Fingers and Ted Simmons to the Milwaukee Brewers for David Green, Dave LaPoint, Sixto Lezcano and Lary Sorensen.

Having one of the best mustaches in major league history, Pete was primarily a reliever before being acquired by the Cardinals. His 2.54 ERA for a poor 1978 team was third best in the National League. An intimidating presence on the mound due to his demonstrative routines, Vuckovich enjoyed 12, 15 and 12 win seasons with a cumulative 3.21 ERA with the team. His first season with the Brewers was rewarded with Cy Young accolades based on his 18-6 record even though he gave up more hits than innings pitched. A rotator cuff injury derailed his career in 1983, resulting in only 8 more wins before retiring in 1986. He finished his 11 year career with a 93-69 record and 3.66 ERA

Pete became part of the Brewers television crew from 1989-1991 before enjoying twenty years in the Pittsburgh organization, including the Pirates pitching coach from 1997-2000. In 2012, Pete moved to Seattle to become special assistant to the general manager with the Mariners, a position he also held in Pittsburgh.

Tom Walker

- February 3, 1976: Purchased by the St. Louis Cardinals from the Detroit Tigers.
- March 24, 1977: Released by the St. Louis Cardinals.

Owner of a 15 inning no-hitter in the minors in 1971, Walker pitched in 10 games with the Cardinals in 1976 covering 19 2/3 innings with a 1-2 record and 4.12 ERA. It was what happened, or never happened four years before. A teammate of Roberto Clemente in 1972 winter ball, Tom assisted Roberto loading the plane on its mission to aid earthquake-torn Nicaragua. Walker was ready to assist unloading the plane as well, prompting Roberto to turn down the offer and enjoy New Year's in Puerto Rico with family. The plane went down, killing Clemente. "He saved my life by not letting me get on the plane," notes Walker.

Tom ended his major league run in 1977 with a 6 year mark of 18-23, getting involved in Whisky sales then the healthcare industry, quite a stretch from whisky sales! Proud father of Neil, an infielder for the Pirates, Walker is now employed at Nemshoff Healthcare Furniture in Pennsylvania.

Mike Wallace

- June 13, 1975: Purchased by the St. Louis Cardinals from the New York Yankees.
- October 22, 1976: Traded by the St. Louis Cardinals to the Texas Rangers for John Sutton.

How does a relief pitcher, a lefty at that, get sold after a 6-0 record and 2.41 ERA in 1974? That is what happened with Mike Wallace, acquired by the Redbirds in June 1975. One of a handful of pitchers to throw a complete game in their major league debut (his only one of his career), Mike pitched in 58 games in '75 and '76 for the Cards, all in relief. After a spotty 1976 season with a 4.07 ERA Wallace was dealt to Texas, where he ended his major league career the following season.

After a career as a sales executive, Mike began working as a baseball pundit for the Mid-Atlantic Sports Network as well as hosting "Nats Talk," a weekend show focusing on the Washington Nationals.

Steve Waterbury

- Before 1971 Season: Signed by the St. Louis Cardinals as an amateur free agent.
- June 15, 1977: Traded by the St. Louis Cardinals with Bake McBride to the Philadelphia Phillies for Rick Bosetti, Dane Iorg and Tom Underwood.

A Carbondale, Illinois native and eight-year minor league veteran, Waterbury pitched in 5 games at the end of the 1976 season totaling 6 innings with a 6.00 ERA. He never pitched in the big leagues thereafter, ending his professional career after the conclusion of the 1978 season.

Steve still resides in Southern Illinois, where he has been self- employed in the consumer electronics business.

Stan Williams

- September 1, 1971: Traded by the Minnesota Twins to the St. Louis Cardinals for players to be named later. The St. Louis Cardinals sent Fred Rico (September 14, 1971) and Dan Ford (minors) (September 14, 1971) to the Minnesota Twins to complete the trade.
- April 9, 1972: Released by the St. Louis Cardinals.

Williams, a 14 year veteran, appeared in ten games with the Cards in September 1971 pitching very well in relief and compiling a 3-0 record and 1.42 ERA. "Big Daddy," a 6'5" presence on the mound won between 14 & 15 games each season between 1960 & 1962 and had his best year in 1970 in Minnesota as a reliever compiling a 10-1 record and 1.99 ERA.

Williams stayed in baseball as a pitching coach after his career ended, coaching for 14 seasons in Boston, New York (A), Seattle, Chicago (A) and Cincinnati. He later scouted for the Tampa and Washington organizations.

Rick Wise

- February 25, 1972: Traded by the Philadelphia Phillies to the St. Louis Cardinals for Steve Carlton.
- October 26, 1973: Traded by the St. Louis Cardinals with Bernie Carbo to the Boston Red Sox for Reggie Smith and Ken Tatum

Acquired for Steve Carlton before the 1972 season, many suggested the deal was even for both sides. An 18-year old Rick Wise had pitched the 2nd game of the doubleheader for the Phillies in 1964 just after Jim Bunning threw a perfect game in the first. Wise won his first game that day, a three hitter, the first of 188 games he would win in his 18 year career. He also threw a no-hitter in 1971, hitting two home runs during the game.

As we all know, Carlton won 329 games, 2 World Series titles and 4 Cy Young awards.

Wise did have a fine two seasons with the Cardinals, winning 16 games each season, along with 5 shutouts in 1973. The team was looking for more hitting, so Wise was dispatched to Boston after the season, where he appeared in his only World Series with the Red Sox in 1975.

After his retirement as a player during the 1982 season, Wise began a twenty year coaching career at every level in the minor leagues along with managing Lancaster of the Atlantic League in 2007.

Joel Youngblood

- March 28, 1977: Traded by the Cincinnati Reds to the St. Louis Cardinals for Bill Caudill.
- June 15, 1977: Traded by the St. Louis Cardinals to the New York Mets for Mike Phillips.

A rightfielder with a rifle arm, Youngblood, winning a World Series title with the Reds in 1976, finished second to Cardinal George Hendrick in outfield assists in 1979. His time with the Redbirds was brief,

27 at bats, 1 RBI and a .185 average in 1977. Upon his acquisition by the Mets, player-manager Joe Torre retired as a player to free up a spot for him. Joel enjoyed his best seasons as a Met, hitting .275 & .276 during the 1979 and 1980 seasons. He made the All Star game in 1981 based on an injury-plagued .350 season.

Youngblood's claim to fame is that he is the only player in major league history to get hits for two different teams in two different cities on the same day. After getting a hit in Chicago off Hall of Famer Ferguson Jenkins, the Met was traded to Montreal after the game. Joel hopped a plane to Philadelphia and singled off another Hall of Famer, Steve Carlton.

After his 14 year career ended in 1989 with a .265 average, Youngblood remained in coaching for the Cincinnati, Milwaukee and Baltimore organizations. After a seven year run in computer sales, Joel returned to the Arizona organization as a third base coach with the Diamondbacks in 2010 and currently is a base running/bunting instructor in the minor leagues.

Chris Zachary

- July 1, 1970: Traded by the Kansas City Royals to the St. Louis Cardinals for Ted Abernathy.
- December 7, 1971: Traded by the St. Louis Cardinals to the Detroit Tigers for Bill Denehy.

Zachary, who once described himself as being "a pretty decent 10th man on a 10-man staff," started 12 games with the Cardinals in 1971 compiling a 3-10 record and 5.32 ERA. His finest work in the majors was the following season with Detroit, helping them win a divisional title with a 1.41 ERA in 25 games. His professional career ended in 1974. Chris passed away in 2003 after a long battle with bone cancer at the age of 59.

Bart Zeller

- Before 1963 Season: Signed by the St. Louis Cardinals as an amateur free agent.
- June 8, 1970: Released by the St. Louis Cardinals.

The "Moonlight Graham" (Field of Dreams film) of the modern era, Zeller appeared in one game with the Cardinals in 1970, catching one inning, and recording one putout on a strikeout by Billy McCool. No trips to the plate followed-EVER! On deck a few times that season, the inning always ended before he got his chance. His career ended the following season due to knee cartilage damage by a slide by future major leaguer Don Baylor. Bart went into marketing before baseball called him back again.

After managing stints with Sioux Falls and Southern Illinois (Marion), Bart was named manager of the inaugural Joliet Slammers of the Frontier League. Manager of the Year in the league his first season, Zeller now coaches and instructs a winter league team in California.

Fast Stats: HITS

BROCK	1617
SIMMONS	1550
REITZ	892
TORRE	888
HERNANDEZ	676
TEMPLETON	654
SIZEMORE	650
TYSON	616
McBRIDE	439
MUMPHREY	434

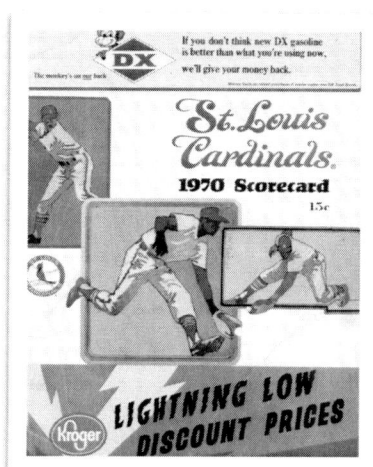

1970

76-86 13 GB 4th Place

Winning their fewest games since 1959 the Cardinals of 1970 were never in contention losing 17 out of 19 in July (8-21 during the month) at one point. The offense perked up over the previous season, scoring 149 more runs, but the shaky pitching allowed 207 more runs.

The good news: hitting. Torre and Brock enjoyed seasons over .300, Dick Allen slugged 34 home runs, the most by a Cardinal since Stan Musial in 1954, and Jose Cardenal added 26 stolen bases. Bob Gibson enjoyed his last great season on the mound, winning the Cy Young Award based on his 23-7 record and 3.12 ERA.

The bad news: pitching. Other than Gibson, the pitching was poor. Carlton dropped to 10-19, no other starter won more than 8 games, the bullpen was ineffective, the team ERA was 4.05. In addition, Mike Shannon's career was cut short at the age of 30 due to kidney disease. The road to the top suddenly got a lot steeper.

1971

90-72 7 GB 2nd Place

Fifth in the majors in wins, the Cardinals bounced back from the previous season winning 14 more games. Leading the league in hitting, the pitching, particularly the starting staff, improved over the 1970

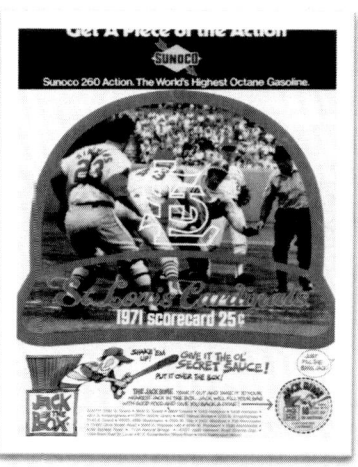

ter. If not for another miserable month of June (8-21), the Redbirds could have made it a lot more interesting down the stretch.

Lead by Joe Torre and his MVP season (.363, 137 RBI's), Simmons, Alou and Brock all batted over .300. Gibson pitched a no-hitter against the Pirates and won 16, Carlton rebounded to win 20, and Moe Drabowsky added some stability in the bullpen. The future started to look much brighter.

1972

75-81 21½ GB 4th Place

Steve Carlton traded, Jerry Reuss traded, the strike-ridden season had not even started before the Cardinals suffered significant loss. It did not get improve either. The bullpen was ineffective until the arrival of Diego Segui, the defense was mediocre and the team scored 171 runs less than 1971. Scipio Spinks, acquired in the Reuss trade, suffered a career-damaging knee injury after winning 5 games, Joe Torre dropped 74 points in batting.

On the bright side, Simmons, Alou and Brock all had seasons over .300; the starting staff, lead by Gibson, Wise and Cleveland won 19, 16 and 14 games respectively. The youth movement began, with the Cardinals dispatching their longtime infield duo of Maxvill and Javier, leaving Brock as the sole survivor of the El Birdo years of the late sixties.

1973

81-81 1½ GB 2nd Place

After their worst start in history, losing 12 of the first 13 and 15 out of 20, the Cards looked hopeless. Poor defense plagued the team.

However, once Mike Tyson was installed at shortstop, things began to happen- good things. By August, the team was five games in front and eleven games over the .500 mark. Yet erratic pitching and erratic hitting did them in, losing eight in a row and 11 out of 12.

The offense was choppy throughout the season, finishing eighth in the league in scoring. Simmons, Brock, and Sizemore had good seasons, however Torre showed signs of slowing down. Rick Wise won 16, surprise Alan Foster won 13, while an injured Gibson dropped to 12 wins. The bullpen became effective with the likes of Segui, Folkers, Pena and Hrabosky. One of the greatest comebacks from the worst start in team history fell just short.

1974

86-75 1½ GB

Another disappointing finish, the Redbirds could not close out the charging Pirates in late September. After holding a 2 1/2 game lead on the 17th, the Cards went 6-7 the rest of the way while the Pirates surged to take the title.

The outfield of Brock with his record-breaking (at the time) 118 stolen bases, McBride, and Smith both at .309 provided an extremely productive outfield. Sizemore, batting second, was the catalyst for Brock's thefts. At third, the Zamboni, Ken Reitz, stopped everything in his path. While the bullpen was solid for a second consecutive season earning 18 saves (do not scoff-Montreal lead the league with 27 saves), the starters struggled. While McGlothen turned in a solid season, winning 16 games Gibson fell to 11-13, and Foster to 7-10. There would be no more races for the Cardinals this close again for the rest of the decade.

1975

82-80   -10½ GB 4TH Place

Struggling early in the season, the Cardinals finally got within distance of the Pirates in mid-August, closing within two games of first. From August 27 through the end of the season the Cards collapsed, closing at 12-21, falling to fourth place, 10 1/2 games out.

The offense continued to be effective, though erratic. McBride, Brock, Smith and Simmons all batted over .300. Newcomers Ron Fairly and Willie Davis helped as well. The defense was erratic however, and Ed Brinkman was disappointing at shortstop.

Forsch and McGlothen both enjoyed 15 win seasons and Hrabosky enjoyed a great season out of the pen, closing with a 13-3 record, 1.67 ERA and 22 saves, earning the Sporting News Fireman of the Year Award. The pitching was good until the late August-September collapse. We said goodbye to the great Bob Gibson, closing out a Hall of Fame career with a 3-11 record.

1976

72-90   -29 GB 5th Place

Kerplunk! A poor year plagued by poor defense, injuries, inconsistent pitching and a mediocre bullpen that cost manager Red Schoendienst his job at the conclusion of the season.

Brock and Willie Crawford, who would depart at the end of the season, were the only starters over the .300 mark. (Unless one counts McBride, who batted .335, in only 72 games). The lone power source, Smith, was dealt to LA for another catcher named Joe Ferguson they did not need. This was, of course, the beginning of the free agent era. The trades and injuries did make way for young hitters Mumphrey and Templeton.

Only Denny and McGlothen reached double figures in wins, and Hrabosky dropped off from his stellar season the year before. Even the Cardinals bicentennial pillbox hats could do them no good this year.

1976 St. Louis Cardinals

1977

83-79   -18 GB 3rd Place

The new sheriff in town, Vern Rapp, was a strict disciplinarian with ties to the Cincinnati Reds organization- ie: no facial hair, no long hair. His policy and demeanor, initially backed by ownership, caused strife in the clubhouse with Hrabosky, McBride, Simmons and even Brock having confrontations with him. In spite of this, the Redbirds improved from the horrid season of 1976; at one point the team was 16 games over .500.

Lead by fine seasons from Brock, Simmons and Templeton and the return of Reitz, the club finished fourth in the league in batting, but defense was too inconsistent.

Forsch won 20 for the only time in his career, Rasmussen won 11, but lost 17. Denny, newly acquired Larry Dierker and Falcone had poor seasons and the bullpen was brutal at times, especially Hrabosky and Eastwick. By the start of the following season, both McBride and "The Mad Hungarian" were gone.

1978

69-93   -21 GB 5th Place

" We Can Do It"

We can light up your day
And thrill you at night
Put a smile on your face
and make you feel all right

Come on Cardinals
Victory time is here
Hey, St. Louis, stand up with a cheer

There's nothing to it, we can do it
Hey, St. Louis, we can do it

The above song was played every game from the opener until it was obvious they indeed could not do it, sometime in Mid-May. By that time, Rapp had been fired after calling Simmons "a loser." Ex - Cardinal Ken Boyer took over in late April and experienced a 12 game losing streak the following month.

The offense was, well, offensive; no hitter reached the .290 mark. The team scored 133 less runs than the season before and had a 23-44 record against left handed pitchers. Templeton, while reaching a lot of balls no other shortstop could reach, finished with a league high 40 errors (league leader Bowa had 10).

The pitching was better than 1977: Denny won 14, Vukovich 12 and Forsch 11, against 17 losses. Bob also pitched the first of his two career no-hitters, and Martinez gave the team a fresh arm with nine victories. Boyer was re-hired. However, the Cardinal career of General Manager Bing Devine came to an end.

1979

86-76   -12 GB   3rd Place

Rebounding from a .221 1978 season, Brock finished his excellent career at .304, as well as recording his 3000 hit AND breaking the all-time stolen base record (at the time). "I wanted to go out in a blaze of glory," noted Lou. Four others batted over .300 including Co-MVP Hernandez, Hendrick, newcomer Oberkfell and Templeton, who had 100 hits from each side of the plate. Simmons was slowed by a broken bone in his wrist.

The starters were good, lead by Vukovich and Martinez, who each won 15, along with Forsch with 11 and Fulgham with 10 wins. Other than Littell, the bullpen was mediocre, costing the team numerous games.

The decade drew to a close. Much better days were just around the corner.

Fast Stats: RBI's

SIMMONS	828
BROCK	481
TORRE	457
REITZ	396
HERNANDEZ	328
TYSON	238
SIZEMORE	230
TEMPLETON	205
SMITH	199
HENDRICK	142

★ *First Round Cardinal Draft Picks 1970-1979* ★

1970-Jim Browning-Made AA in Philadelphia organization, career minor league mark of 26-23, 3.64 over six seasons

1971-Ed Kurpiel- AAA with numerous organizations, 10 seasons, .252 average, 100 homers

1972-Dan Larson-Parts of seven seasons in the majors with Houston, Philadelphia & Cubs, 10-25 record, 4.40 ERA

1973-Joe Edelen-1-0 with Cards in 1981, 1-0 with Cincinnati in 1981, career 6.75 ERA, nine seasons in minors

1974-Garry Templeton-16 year major league veteran, career .271 average, 242 stolen bases, 3 time All Star

1975-Dave Johnson-Seven seasons in minors, AA with Cardinals, 42-34 career mark, 3.55 ERA

1976-Leon Durham-10 year major league veteran, .277 career average, 147 Homers, 2 time All Star

1977-Terry Kennedy-14 year major league career-.264 average, 113 homers, 4 time All Star

1978-Robert Hicks-Seven seasons in minors, high as AA in Texas organization, career .237 average, 53 homers

1979-Andy Van Slyke-13 year major league career-.274 average, 164 homers, 245 stolen bases, 3 time All Star

Fast Stats: HOME RUNS

SIMMONS	151
TORRE	80
REITZ	53
SMITH	50
HERNANDEZ	49
BROCK	47
ALLEN	34
HENDRICK	33
HAGUE	33
J. CRUZ	26

★ *The Best Trades of the Decade* ★

1. Jerry DaVanon to Baltimore for Moe Drabowsky 1970

   Certainly no earth-shaker, but the veteran reliever added some much needed stability to a shaky bullpen during that time with a 6-1 record and eight saves in 1971, not to mention his antics in the bullpen. DaVanon lasted eight years in the bigs, batting a career .234 before returning to the Cardinals not once, but two more times.

2. Joe Hague to Cincinnati for Bernie Carbo 1972

   Carbo added some punch to the lineup in 1972 & '73, including a .286 mark with 40 ribbies in 1973. Hague ended his career in 1973, including a .228 mark in his two seasons with the Reds. Trade downgraded when Carbo was re-acquired in 1979 and introduced Cardinal slugger Keith Hernandez to recreational drugs.

3. Purchased Alan Foster from California 1973

   Foster provided a boost to the starting staff in 1973, winning 13 with a 3.14 ERA. He dropped in effectiveness the following season (7-10 3.88) before moving on. Still does not cancel out the sale of Cruz to Houston the following year.

4. Rick Wise and Bernie Carbo for Reggie Smith and Ken Tatum 1973

   A deal that worked for both teams, Wise won another 81 games before hanging them up. Carbo had some terrific moments with the Sox, including Game 6 of the 1975 World Series, but Smith added a much-needed punch to the Cards lineup as well as good defense. He hit .293 and hit 50 homers in his two and a half seasons with the Redbirds. Tatum never made it out of the minors with the Cards before being traded the following year.

5. Reggie Cleveland, Diego Segui and Terry Hughes to Boston for Lynn McGlothen, John Curtis and Mike Garman 1973

   Another even deal with the Bosox. Cleveland won another 65 games after leaving the Cards, Segui had 16 saves in the next two seasons, Hughes batted .203 in 69 at bats in 1974. McGlothen won 44 with the Redbirds, the lefty Curtis 24 and Garman won 10 with 16 saves.

6. Rudy Kinard & Ed Kurpiel for Ron Fairly 1974
    Fairly supplied some defense as well as some punch, batting .289 with a .409 OBP during his year and a half with the organization. Neither Kinard or Kurpiel reached the majors.

7. Ed Brinkman and Tommy Moore to Texas for Willie Davis 1975
    Davis batted .291 with 6 homers and 50 RBI's in his half season with the Cardinals, a washed up Brinkman was quickly dealt to the Yankees where he hit .175. Moore won two major league games with Seattle in 1977.

8. Mark Covert for Buddy Schultz 1977
    Schultz, a hard-throwing lefty out of the pen, was 12-8 with 10 saves over three seasons. Injuries derailed his career however. Covert made it as far as AA ball.

9. Tom Underwood & Victor Cruz to Toronto for Pete Vuckovich & John Scott 1977
    On the surface, this does not look like such a good deal. Underwood won another 52 games in his career and Cruz had a five year run in the majors, saving 37 games. Vuckovich won 79 games after the trade, 39 of them with the Cardinals. His commanding presence on the mound enabled him to win 24 games with two poor Cardinal teams (1978 & 1980). Scott never reached the majors again.

10. Eric Rasmussen to San Diego for George Hendrick 1978
    Rasmussen won another 26 games (and lost 38) before his career ended in 1983.
 Hendrick hit .294 over his seven seasons with the club, with 122 homers and nearly 1000 hits.

Fast Stats: STOLEN BASES

BROCK	551
TEMPLETON	99
McBRIDE	75
MUMPHREY	66
SCOTT	55
CARDENAL	38
HERNANDEZ	35
ALOU	30
SIZEMORE	27
J. CRUZ	23

★ *Worst Trades of the Decade (In Chronological Order)* ★

1.   Cookie Rojas to Kansas City for Fred Rico   1970
     Rojas batted .268 over 8 seasons with K.C. earning four All-Star berths. He paved the way for Frank White to take over in 1976. Rico reached AAA Tulsa, but not the majors after a short stent with the expansion Royals in 1969.

2.   Mike Torrez to Montreal for Bob Reynolds 1971
     Torrez won 164 games after leaving the Redbirds, including a World Series title with New York in 1977. Reynolds pitched in four games with Cards in 1971 covering seven innings, and later had some success with Baltimore in 1973-'74.

3.   Steve Carlton to Philadelphia for Rick Wise 1972
     It was not the fact that Wise was bad; he won 16 games each of his two seasons with the Cardinals, including a All Star selection. It was the fact that the lefty Carlton was so darn good, winning 252 after the trade, including four Cy Young Awards and 27 games with a poor '72 Phillies team. One of the two left-handers who got away.

4.   Jerry Reuss to Houston for Scipio Spinks and Lance Clemons 1972
     Reuss won 198 games after leaving St. Louis, including two All Star selections. Spinks looked promising before injuring his knee. He won six games for the club in 1972-'73, his last in the majors. Clemons appeared in three games in 1972 with one loss; he won a total of two major league games.

5.   Jim Bibby to Texas for Mike Nagy and John Wockenfuss 1973
     Bibby won 110 games after leaving the Cardinals, including a World Series ring and All Star selection. Nagy pitched in 9 games for the Redbirds in 1973; his major league career ended the following sea-

son. Wockenfuss enjoyed a 12 year major league career, though none of it for the Cards.

6.   Cruz sold to Houston 1974
   I know it is not a trade, but Jose had almost 2000 hits for the Astros, a bad one for the Cards.

7.   Larry Herndon and Luis Gonzalez to San Francisco for Ron Bryant 1975
   Herndon enjoyed a 14- year career, winning a title with Detroit in 1984, batting .274 with over 1300 hits. Gonzalez never made it past AAA. Bryant pitched in 8, count em 8 games for the Cards in 1975 covering 8 innings with a 16.62 ERA. 'Nuff said.

8.   Reggie Smith for Fred Tisdale, Bob Detherage and Joe Ferguson 1976
   Free agency played a part in this deal The Redbirds feared Reggie's contract demands would be too great. He played another 7 seasons, 6 with the Dodgers batting a cumulative .297 with 115 homers. Tisdale went as far as AAA, Detherage had 26 major league at bats, none with the Cardinals. Ferguson batted a measly .201 in half a season before moving on in another deal.

9.   Mike Easler to California for a player to be named later, Ron Farkas was that player. 1976
   Easler never reached beyond AAA with the Cardinals even though the "Hit Man" batted over .300 with Tulsa in 1975 & 1976. He enjoyed a 14 year career in the majors, primarily with Pittsburgh, hitting a career .293. Farkas never reached past AAA status.

10. Jerry Mumphrey and John Denny for Bobby Bonds 1979
   This might be saving the worst for last. Mumphrey enjoyed another 10 seasons in the bigs, hitting over .300 in four of them including an All Star selection. Denny won another 72 games, a World Series Ring (1980) and a Cy Young Award (1983). Bonds, limited by a hand injury, batted .203 in 1980 before being released at the conclusion of that retched season.

In the decade of the 1970's, the Cardinals traded Steve Carlton, Jerry Reuss, Mike Torrez and Jim Bibby. Those four combined to win 730 games (count em) after leaving the club. The pitchers the Redbirds received in return for the quartet won 38, yes 38 games with the team, never finding an adequate left-handed starter (much less two) to replace two of the best of the decade.

Fast Stats: SHUTOUTS

GIBSON	14
FORSCH	12
DENNY	10
McGLOTHEN	9
CLEVELAND	8
WISE	7
CARLTON	6
RASMUSSEN	6
REUSS	4
MARTINEZ	4

STRIKEOUTS

GIBSON	998
FORSCH	524
CLEVELAND	445
DENNY	409
McGLOTHEN	394
HRABOSKY	385
CARLTON	365
VUKOVICH	294
WISE	286
RASMUSSEN	285

SAVES

HRABOSKY	59
SEGUI	26
LITTELL	24
GARMAN	16
TAYLOR	11
SCHULTZ	11
DRABOWSKY	10
PENA	7
METZGER	7
2 TIED WITH	6

★ Bibliography ★

Baseball-reference.com
baseball-almanac.com
Sabr.org
Historic Baseball.com
rangerscards.blogspot
baseball1976.blogspot.com
mlb.com
fanbase.com
wgom.org
75toppsblogspot.com
astrosdaily.com
blog.buhner.com
colorado.rockies.mlb.com
findagrave.com
texas.rangers.mlb.com
tampabay.rays.mlb.com
blogs.cjonline.com
reocities.com
1978topps.blogspot.com
retrosheet.org
deadspin.com
baseballthinkfactory.org
1986toppsblogspot.com
dugoutdug.blogspot.com
fleersticker.blogspot.com
njbaseball.blogspot.com
stlouis.cardinals.mlb.com
greatest21days.com
seattle.mariners.mlb.com

ultimatemets.com
retrosimba.com
classicminnesotatwins.blogspot.com
baseballblogspot.com
speakingofsports.com
majorleagueadventures.com
1980toppsbaseball.blogspot.com
centerfieldmaz.com
chicagocubscards.com
statsheet.com
espn.go.com
Royals.mlblogs.com
1977topps.blogspot.com
baseball.org
linkedin.com
1965topps.blogspot.com
newyorkyankees.mlb.com
archives.starbulletin.com
sculu.com
thedeadballera.com
ontheoutsidecorner.wordpress.com
1974topps-pennantfever.blogspot
chicago.whitesox.mlb.com
pabaseball.blogspot.com
oriolescards.blogspot.com
sfgate.com
zoominfo.com
Factbites.com
marinersblog.mlblogs.com

bleedingyankeeblue.blogspot.com
The Sporting News Baseball Guides 1971-1980
greatorioleautographproject.blogspot.com
baseballbytheletters.blogspot.com

Abernathy	SABR.org Bob Hurte The Sporting News- 7/25/70 Sid Bordman
Agee	SABR.org Mark Armour
Allen, Dick	Hardballtimes.com 12/18/09 Bruce Markusen Hallofverygood.com 7/9/12 Andrew Woolley
Allen, Ron	ysusports.com 8/18/10 The Sporting News 8/26/72 Neal Russo
Alou	SABR.org Mark Armour Baseballguru.com Bruce Markusens page
Alvarado	The Sporting News 6/15/74 Neal Russo
Alyea	Sports Illustrated-A New Land, An Old Bond 6/30/86 Peter Gammons
Anderson, Dwain	kennethsuskin.blogspot.com 7/5/10 Kenneth Suskin The Sporting News 10/7/72 Neal Russo
Andrew	The Sporting News 2/10/73, 4/7/73 Neal Russo
Alyala	Sportsillustrated.cnn.com 7/12/82 Steve Wulf Voices.yahoo.com 9/25/10 Stephen Sullivan
Bare	blessyouboys.com 1/24/13 Al Beaton
Barlow	cardboardgods.net 6/16/08 Highbeam.com Syracuse New Times 5/28/03 Justin Park The Sporting News 6/17/75 Regis McAuley
Beauchamp	thedeadballera.com 12/27/07 AP
Bertaina	legacy.com fishinginternational.com The Sporting News 10/10/70 Jerome Holtzman

The Sporting News 4/24/71 Neal Russo

Bibby   Sportsillustrated.cnn.com 2/18/10 Joe Posnanski

Billings   Sportsillustrated.cnn.com 4/19/10 Joe Posnanski

Bosetti   ci.redding.ca.us

Bradford   articles.latimes.com 7/2/94Fernando Dominguez
               The Sporting News 12/20/75 Neal Russo

Briles   MLB.com 2/13/05 Ed Eagle

Brinkman   USAtoday30.usatoday.com 10/3/08
               hardballtimes.com 1/6/12 Bruce Markusen
               The Sporting News 12/7/74 Neal Russo

Brunet   mininggazette.com 5/22/10 Paul Peterson
               hardballtimes.com 1/18/05 Steve Treder
               bleacherreport.com 12/2/09 Andrew Godfrey

Bruno   articles.aberdeennews.com 4/17/11 John Papendick
               aglr.wordpress.com 5/2/11 Brittany Grome
               The Sporting News 5/12/79 Rick Hummel

Bryant   The Sporting News 4/19/75 Pat Frizzell
               The Sporting News 5/31/75 Neal Russo

Burda   The Sporting News 5/1/71 Neal Russo
               The Sporting News 5/6/72 John Wilson

Busse   The Sporting News 12/16/72 John Wilson
               The Sporting News 12/16/72 Neal Russo

D Campbell   SABR-Alex Kupfer

Campisi   The Sporting News 11/7/70 Bob Fowler

Capilla   The Sporting News 5/28/77 Neal Russo

Carbo	SABR-Andrew Blume
	The Sporting News 10/26/01 Andy Clendenen
Carlton	Stevecarlton.com
	voices.yahoo.com 9/24/08 Harold Friend
Cardenal	Bleedcubbieblue.com Al Yellon
	The Sporting News 8/21/71 Larry Whiteside
Carroll	ashof.org
	The Sporting News 6/6/77 Neal Russo
Cater	articles.sun-sentinel 8/14/85 Ira Winderman
Chant	The Sporting News 11/29/75 Neal Russo
Chlupsa	gojaspers.com
Clarey	SABR-Joe Schuster
	billy-ball.com 3/5/13 Bill Chuck
Clemons	deadballera.com 1/25/08
	www.tampabay.com 3/13/08
Clendenon	SABR-Ed Hoyt
	risingapple.com 11/30/12 Matt Musico
Cleveland	SABR-Maurice Bouchard
	Boston Globe 12/8/73 Peter Gammons
Cloninger	News@norman.com 10/6/01 Tyson C. Leonhardt
Coluccio	articles.latimes.com 11/29/91 Tom Hamilton
	mlb.com 5/21/11 Roger Schlueter
Crawford	LA Times 8/29/04 Ben Bolch
	The Sporting News 3/20/76 Gordon Verrell
	The Sporting News 11/6/76 Neal Russo
Crosby	Sfgate.com 8/20/04 Susan Slusser
	Presstelegram.com 9/17/10

T Cruz   seattlemariners.mlb.com 1/13/09 Jim Street
The Sporting News 9/22/77 Neal Russo

H Cruz   The Sporting News 12/24/77 Richard Dozer

J Cruz   houston.astros.mlb.com 7/19/12 Brian McTaggart

Culver   i70baseball.com 11/25/11 Bob Netherton
seamheads.com Dave Heller

Curtis   baseballsavvy.com John Curtis
The Sporting News 11/6/76 Neal Russo
Sports Illustrated "Has Typewriter, Will Pitch"
5/12/80 Ron Fimrite

D'Acquisto   nytimes.com 10/18/96
chickenfriars.com 7/14/12 Robert Moreno
The Sporting News 5/28/77 Neal Russo

Davalillo   SABR-Rory Costello
The Sporting News 10/3/70 Neal Russo

DaVanon   Astrosdaily.com 8/31/05 Willie B. Lakey
The Sporting News 12/11/76 Neal Russo

Davis   latimesblogs.latimes 3/9/10 Andrew Blankstein
The Sporting News 6/28/75 Neal Russo

Denny   People.com 4/9/84 Richard K. Rein
memphismagazine.com May 2007 Frank Murtaugh
memphisflyer.com 4/19/07 Greg Akers

Dierker   climbingtalshill.com 3/23/13 Greg Thurston
The Sporting News 12/11/76 Neal Russo

Dimmel   sportsillustrated.cnn.com 4/30/79 Jim Kaplan

Dressler   Oregonrose.com

Duncan	Sacramento Bee 1/5/04 Mark McDermott
Durham	Theycallitbaseball.blogspot.com 8/11/2001 Bryce Martin
Dwyer	nbc-2.com 12/10/12 Fort Myers The Sporting News 7/1/78 Neal Russo
Eastwick	bronxbanter.baseballtoaster.com 4/11/08 Bruce Markusen
Fairly	SABR-Paul Hirsch The Sporting News 9/25/76 Neal Russo
Falcone	nydailynews.com 5/14/11 Wayne Coffey articles.latimes.com 9/3/94 Steve Elling The Sporting News 7/16/77 & 12/23/78 Neal Russo
Fenwick	SABR-Rory Costello
Ferguson	The Sporting News 7/3/76 Neal Russo
Fisher	Newsok.com 8/16/08 Berry Tramel baseballtoddsdugout.com Todd Newville The Sporting News 11/10/73 Neal Russo
Folkers	WCF Courier-Cedar Valley 3/27/11 Jim Sullivan
Forsch	170baseball.com 3/13/12 Michael Metzger
Foster	Cardboardgods.net 2/23/12 Josh Wilker The Sporting News 4/21 & 4/28/73 Neal Russo
Frazer	nytimes.com 6/26/11 Tyler Kepner tulsapeople.com March 2012 Doug Eaton
Freed	The Sporting News 8/8/81 Stan Isle
Frisella	SABR-Greg Spira

Fulgham	articles.orlandosentinel.com 5/16/93 Jill Cousins
	investing.businessweek.com 4/22/13
	Evening Independent 6/21/80
Garman	Idahopress.com 6/5/11 Tom Fox
	The Sporting News 11/15/75 Neal Russo
	The Sporting News 9/23/78 Ian MacDonald
Garrett	SABR-Les Masterson
Gibson	Bleacherreport.com 11/19/11 Harold Friend
Godby	SABR-John Wickline
Granger	I70baseball.com 3/2/11 Bob Netherton
	The Sporting News 8/25/73 Neal Russo
Greif	SABR-Gregory Wolf
	thecancerconnection.org
	The Sporting News 6/5/76 Neal Russo
Guerrero	Boston.com Boston Globe 5/4/04 Gordon Edes
	The Sporting News 7/12/ 75 Neal Russo
Grzenda	"The Ultimate Closer" 10/25/04 Washington Post
	William Gidea
Guzman	Urbanshocker.wordpress.com 9/9/07
	Malcolm Allen
Hague	The Sporting News 6/3/72 Neal Russo
	The Sporting News 6/30/73 Earl Lawson
Hamilton	Sfgate.com 5/14/02 Mitch Stephens
	baseballguru.com Bruce Markusen
	The Sporting News 6/10/78 Neal Russo
Haney	brewcrewball.com 11/19/12 Kyle Lobner
	old.post-gazette.com 6/16/02 Steve Ziants

Harris	The Sporting News 5/29/76 Neal Russo
Heidemann	eastvalleytribune.com 1/31/12 Mike Sakal
Heintzelman	The Sporting News 10/27/73 Neal Russo
Heise	SABR-Bill Nowlin The Sporting News 7/20 & 8/17/74 Neal Russo
Hendrick	newyorker.com 10/22/08 Roger Angell
Hernandez	pauulebowitz.com 11/30/12 The Sporting News 5/10/75 & 6/28/75 Neal Russo
Hernd	espn.go.com 5/20/11 Thomas Neumann motownsports.com 8/20/12 Steve Kornacki mlive.com 7/21/10 Dean Holzwarth
Herr	Lancasteronline.com 11/25/12 Mike Gross The Sporting News 5/9/88 Peter Pascarelli
Hickman	voices.yahoo.com 6/6/06 Carl Kolchak sportslifer.wordpress.com 9/21/08 Jim Peyton The Sporting News 4/13 & 8/3/74 Neal Russo
Higgi	newstribune.com 4/14/13 Adam Stillman
Hill	The Sporting News 10/26/74 Pat Frizzell
Howard	byucougars.com sportsillustrated.cnn.com 12/27/99 ksl.com 11/3/11 Ralph R. Zobell
Hrabosky	alhrabosky.com hardballtimes.com 7/16/10 Bruce Markusen
Hudso	The Sporting News 8/1/73 Merle Henry Ford The Sporting News 2/24/73 Neal Russo

Hughes	rule4draft.com 1/12/13 Jim Vassallo
Hunt	rheba.com baseballsavvy.com 1/14/11 Benjamin Pomeranco
Iorg	byucougars.com
Javier	Naplesnews.com 6/26/09 Adam Fisher articles.latimes.com 2/14/91 Bill Plaschke Julianjavierfoundation.org Dominicanbaseballguy.com 5/31/12 Keith Winters
Johnson	The Sporting News 3/14/70 Bob Broeg The Sporting News 5/23 & 5/30/70 Neal Russo
Jutze	The Sporting News 9/16/72 Neal Russo
J Kennedy	The Sporting News 12/13/69 & 7/25/70 Neal Russo
T Kennedy	Hardballtimes.com 11/25/08 Steve Treder Baseballtucson.com 9/15/12 Andrew Cockrum
Kessinger	Bleedcubbieclue.com 1/7/07 Al Yellon Kessingerrealestate.com The Sporting News 9/25/76 Neal Russo
Knowles	Baseballprospectus.com 9/7/10 David Laurila Baseballguru.com Bruce Markusen The Sporting News 10/27/79 Rick Hummel
Krausse	Delconewsnetwork.com 10/19/10 Rich Pagano Mlb.com 4/5/10 Jordan Schelling Kansascitybaseballhistoricalsociety.com
Kubiak	SABR-Rory Costello The Sporting News 8/21/71 Neal Russo
Kurosaki	nytimes.com 12/25/08 Hugo Kugiya

LaGrow	Lerrint.com
Lee	sacsportshof.com
	articles.latimes.com 1/26/86 UPI
	Baseballsacramento.com 7/22/12 Rich Cabral
Lentine	The Sporting News 9/23/78 Neal Russo
Lersch	The Grand Junction Daily Sentinel 10/12/09
	Kent Mincer
	The Sporting News 10/5/74 Neal Russo
Lintz	The Sporting News 8/16/75 Bob Dunn
	The Sporting News 10/4 & 11/15/75 Neal Russo
Linzy	Bleacherreport.com 1/4/12 Matt David
	The Sporting News 5/27/77 Larry Whiteside
Littell	nuttybuddy.com
	dsbluehawks.com
Lopez	Houston Chronicle 9/24/92 Jayne Custred,
	Neil Hohfeld
Martinez	mwlguide.com
	The Sporting News 11/20/71 & 5/27/72
	Neal Russo
Martinez	theamazingsheastadiumautographproject.blogspot
	11/13/10 Lee Harmon
	The Sporting News 6/7/75 Neal Russo
Maxvill	Baseballguru.com Bruce Markusen
McEnaney	Sports Illustrated 7/17/00 Camille Bersumin
	articles.sun-sentinel.com 7/1/85 Dean Chang
	Palmbeachpost.com 4/10/10 Joe Capozzi
McBride	nytimes.com 2/27/85
	The Sporting News 7/2/77 Neal Russo

McCarver   SABR-Dave Williams
                    stltoday.com 7/15/12 Rick Hummel

McGlothen   I70baseball.com 3/18/11 Bob Netherton

McNertney   cyclones.com
                    The Sporting News 11/18/72 Neal Russo

Mejias   mlb.com 10/31/06 Spencer Fordin

Melendez   The Sporting News 6/5/76 Neal Russo

Metzger   firstpitchstrikeone.com
                    The Sporting News 6/4/77 Neal Russo

Moore   The Sporting News 5/3/75, 10/26/75
                    Neal Russo

Morales   Bleedcubbieblue.com 11/18/06 Al Yellon
                    The Sporting News 5/27/78 Dick Kaegel

Murphy   articles.latimes 11/8/91 Patrick Mott
                    The Sporting News 9/1/73 Neal Russo

Nagy   SABR-Rory Costello
                    The Sporting News 4/21/73 Neal Russo

Norman   The Sporting News 6/19/71 Les Koelling

Nossek   cooloftheevening.com Jim Thielman

Nye   lib.niu.edu 3/20/84 Ted Thomas 3/20/84
                    Nessexoticwellness.com

Oberkfell   thecardinalnationblog.com 12/8/12
                    Brian Walton

O'Brien   emueagles.com

Osteen	SABR-Gregory Wolf
Palmer	The Sporting News 8/26/72 Neal Russo The Sporting News 11/11/72 Russell Schneider
Papi	Pinetarpress.com 7/5/10 Greg Schaum The Sporting News 4/27/74 Neal Russo
Parker	Newsok.com 9/3/12 Scott Munn
Patterson	SABR-Parker Bena cos.edu
Pena	Cubanbeisbol.blogspot.com 11/17/11 Cesar Brioso The Sporting News 7/7/73 & 6/8/74 Neal Russo The Sporting News 5/17/75 Dick Miller
Phillips	infozine.com 1/6/05
Plodinec	Arizonawildcats.com Register-mail.com 7/10/07 Tom Wilson
Proly	The Sporting News 6/25/84
Rader	The Sporting News 5/7, 8/27 & 12/24/77 Neal Russo
Ramirez	The Sporting News 12/2/72 Neal Russo
Ramsey	sptimes.com 7/19/00 Rodney Page
Rasmussen	sportsillustrated.cnn.com 5/2/77 Jim Kaplan The Sporting News 1/1/77, 5/6/78 Neal Russo
Reed	mlb.com 6/7/12 Larry Shenk The Sporting News 7/5/75 Neal Russo

Reitz	Florissant.patch.com 5/27/11
	Keith Schlidroth
Reuss	SABR-Paul Hirsch
	JerryReuss.com
	The Sporting News 4/18/70 Neal Russo
Reynolds	seattlepi.com 7/29/03 Dan Raley
Reynolds	metrowestdailynews.com 6/7/09 Rick Smith
Richard	bruce.mlblogs.com 5/7/09
	Bruce Markusen
	The Sporting News 4/28/79 Richard Dozer
Richert	The Sporting News 6/8/74 Neal Russo
Rojas	I70baseball.com 11/22/11 Bob Netherton
	The Sporting News 4/18/70 Neal Russo
Roque	Thestar.com 12/14/09 Richard Griffin
Rudolph	The Sporting News 4/16/77 Neal Russo
Sadecki	polishsportshof.com
	seamheads.com 10/4/09 Justin Murphy
Santorini	Mlb.com Jennifer Langosch
Scheinblum	The Big Book of Jewish Baseball
	Peter S. & Joachim Horvitz
	The Sporting News 9/21, 11/6/74 Neal Russo
Schofield	old.post-gazette.com 6/13/02 Rich Emert
	stlbeacon.com 11/3/09 Paul Pouse
	The Sporting News 11/7/70 Neal Russo
Schultz	Buddyschultz.com
	Cleveland Plain Dealer 4/5/11 Rachel Dissell

The Sporting News 10/27/79 Rick Hummel

Scott   mjbl.org
                   The Sporting News 9/3/77, 6/9/79 Neal Russo

Segui   SABR-Joanne Hulbert

Shannon   Shannonsteak.com

Shirley   The Sporting News 4/17/82 Rick Hummel

Siebert   SABR-Joseph Wancho
                   The Sporting News 5/4/74 Neal Russo

Simmons   Stltoday.com 9/19/10 Rick Hummel

Sizemore   Latimes.com 6/7/94 David W. Myers
                   The Sporting News 3/20/76 Gordon Verrell

Smith   SABR-Jeff Angus
                   The Sporting News 6/12 & 7/3/76 Neal Russo

Solomon   The Sporting News 6/26/76 Neal Russo

Sosa   jamaicobserver 4/11/10 Livingston Scott
                   The Sporting News 5/31/75 Neal Russo

Sprague   Sportsillustrated.cnn.com 10/26/92 Steve Wulf

Spinks   SABR-Rory Costello
                   The Sporting News 5/27/72 Neal Russo

Stein   Orlando Sentinel 7/7/88 Mike Zizzo

Stinson   The Sporting News 3/7/81 Tracy Ringolsby

Sutton   The Sporting News 4/30/77 Neal Russo
                   The Sporting News 12/24/77 Stan Isle

Swisher   Bleedcubbieblue.com 7/4/11 Al Yellon

Sykes	The Sporting News 12/23/78 Neal Russo The Sporting News 4/19/80 & 11/7/81 Rick Hummel
Tamargo	Jaysjournal.com 1/7/13 Kyle Franzoni
Carl Taylor	articles.orlandosentinel.com 8/18/91 sportsillustrated.com 5/18/02 The Sporting News 1/28/70 Neal Russo
Chuck Taylor	goblueraiders.com theamazingsheastadiumautographproject.blogspot.com 1/3/10 Lee Harmon
Templeton	Jumpsteadytempleton.blogspot.com
Terlecky	sddt.com 1/17/76
Thomas	The Sporting News 8/25/79 Rick Hummel
Thompson	The Sporting News 6/8/74 Neal Russo
Torrez	Boston.com 5/10/05 Jon Goode Kshof.org nydailynews.com 3/26/09 Matt Gagne
Tyson	The Sporting News 4/26/82 Dick Young
Underwood	Kokomotribune.com 11/23/10 Palmbeachpost.com 11/26/10 Hal Habib The Sporting News 7/2/77 Neal Russo The Sporting News 12/24/77 Dick Young
Urrea	thecardinalnationnlog.com Brian Walton The Sporting News 5/7/77 Neal Russo
Vukovich	lookoutlanding.com 9/16/11 Jeff Sullivan bleacherreport.com 5/25/11 Doug Mead

Walker	SABR-Bob Hurte
	The Sporting News 4/16/77 Neal Russo
Wallace	masnsports.com 4/14/11 Phil Wood
	whoislog.info
	The Sporting News 5/15/76 Neal Russo
Williams	seattlepi.com 10/13/03
Wise	SABR-Bill Nowlin
	'75 The Red Sox Team That Saved Baseball
	Bill Nowlin-Cecilia Tan
Youngblood	nydailynews.com 2/21/09 Mark Lelinwalla
	throughthefencebaseball.com 8/16/12 Eric Aron
	The Sporting News 4/16/77 Neal Russo
Zachary	Knoxville News Sentinel 4/21/03
Zeller	Triblocal.com/Joliet 1/25/2011, 3/6/12
	Mary Owen
	The Southern.com 6/9/07 Robert Crow

★ *Special Thanks* ★

Special thanks to Martin Coco and Taka Yanagimoto from the
St. Louis Cardinals organization for their assistance. A big thank you
to Dan Thompson, Jeff Fister and the staff of Bluebird Publishing,
without whose expertise this book would not be possible. Kudos sent
to David Ho for his graphic excellence, and to Susan DeFosset for
her command of the English language. Without all of you, this book
would not exist.